Samuel Cheetham

The mysteries, pagan and Christian

Samuel Cheetham

The mysteries, pagan and Christian

ISBN/EAN: 9783337260446

Printed in Europe, USA, Canada, Australia, Japan

Cover: Foto ©Lupo / pixelio.de

More available books at **www.hansebooks.com**

THE MYSTERIES
PAGAN AND CHRISTIAN

THE MYSTERIES

PAGAN AND CHRISTIAN

BEING THE

HULSEAN LECTURES FOR 1896-97

BY

S. CHEETHAM, D.D., F.S.A.

ARCHDEACON AND CANON OF ROCHESTER
HONORARY FELLOW OF CHRIST'S COLLEGE, CAMBRIDGE
FELLOW AND EMERITUS PROFESSOR OF KING'S COLLEGE, LONDON

London
MACMILLAN AND CO., Limited
NEW YORK: THE MACMILLAN COMPANY
1897

PREFACE

From the time of the revival of learning to the present day the Mysteries of paganism have attracted much notice and been the subjects of much wild theorising, as well as of much scholarly and careful investigation. According to the prepossessions with which they set out, different inquirers have arrived at the most curiously various results, as is natural where the evidence is fragmentary and inconclusive.

The older view of the pagan Mysteries was, that in them was taught an esoteric doctrine, better and nobler than that of the popular religion, which had been handed down from primeval antiquity through a constant succession of priests or hierophants, and imparted from age to age to select votaries who kept the secret of their knowledge. As to the original source of this recondite science opinions varied widely, some deriving it from a primitive revelation to all mankind, some from the Old Testament, some from the hidden wisdom of India or Egypt. Among others, this thesis is maintained by De Sainte Croix in his *Recherches sur les Mystères du Paganisme*, and by Creuzer in his well-known *Symbolik*. Our countryman Warburton held a peculiar theory, that while pagan teachers placed the rewards of goodness in a future world from which no man returned to prove their falsity, Moses alone had the courage to promise to his followers rewards and punishments in this world, in the sight of men. Hence he was led to examine the promises of future retribution given in the Mysteries, and to maintain that they were "the legislator's invention, solely for the propagation and support of the doctrine of a future state of rewards and punishments"—a contention in which he has probably had but few followers. See his *Divine Legation of Moses*, bk. ii. ch. 4.

The fancies and false reasoning of the early inquirers were rudely shaken by the epoch-making work of C. A. Lobeck, which he called

Aglaophamus. In this he examines more particularly the statements of ancient writers with regard to the Eleusinian, the Orphic, and the Samothracian Mysteries, but the book is of the highest importance for the study of the subject generally. In this for the first time all the important authorities are criticised and interpreted by an acute and thoroughly competent scholar, and the statements and theories of such writers as De Sainte Croix and Creuzer (who in this matter largely follows him) are shown to be in many cases utterly baseless. Access to these societies was, he shows, not difficult; they were open to all on easy conditions, without distinction of sex or station; their priests were persons endowed with no extraordinary knowledge, but, in the case of civic Mysteries at least, simple citizens capable of discharging the peculiar ritual with which alone they were concerned. The notion that they propagated a secret doctrine is one borrowed from the East, or from modern ecclesiastical associations, and is utterly alien from classic thought. Lobeck introduced order where all had been chaos, and distinguished where his predecessors had confused; Greek traits were cleared from Oriental, and private separated from public rites. The Orphic Mysteries, for instance, which really belonged to a kind of secret society, were shown to be different in kind from the Eleusinian. It must be confessed, however, that Lobeck treats his subject in too hard and unsympathetic a spirit, tending to ignore the aspirations after higher things than those of the common life which were after all found in the Mysteries.

Ottfried Müller has in several places expressed opinions on the Mysteries by which, even where he is not wholly right, he has thrown much light on the subject. (See his art. "Eleusinia" in Ersch and Gruber's *Encyclop.* i. 33, p. 287 *ff.*, and *Griech. Literatur*, i. 25 and 416 *ff.*) He finds the ground of all mystic rites and associations in the worship of the Chthonian deities. It is this worship, he thinks, that man delights to express in dim symbols and undefined aspirations. This proposition cannot be accepted literally, for other deities besides the Chthonian were worshipped in Mysteries; but it does seem to be true that the doctrines as to the fate of souls in the world to come, which were prominent in the Mysteries, were intimately connected with the worship of the divinities beneath the earth who cause the life of plants and trees.

What is really known of the Mysteries is admirably summarised by L. Preller in his articles on "Eleusinia" and "Mysteria" in Pauly's *Real-Encyclopädie*, which I have found lucid and trustworthy guides in the intricacies of a perplexed subject matter. There are also many suggestive observations on the Mysteries in his *Griechische* and *Römische Mythologie*. In the more recent works which I have consulted I have rarely found reason to depart from Preller's conclusions. Excellent brief histories of them are found also in Maury's *Histoire des Religions de la Grèce antique* (tom. ii.), and in Döllinger's *Heidenthum und Judenthum*, pp. 108 *ff*., 385 *ff*., 447, 498.

Many able writers have discussed the question, how far were Christian Institutions influenced by the pagan Mysteries. Isaac Casaubon, in his *Exercitationes* (p. 478 *ff*. ed. Genev. 1655), points out that the terminology of the Mysteries was received into the Church, and maintains that the form of various Christian ceremonies was to some extent determined by those already existing in paganism. The natural tendency of men to cling to use and wont in matters of religion accounts, he thinks, for the early Christians adopting well-known terms and rites with a changed significance. In the controversies of the seventeenth century as to the hypothesis of a system of dogmas secretly handed down in the Church from the days of our Lord—the so-called "Disciplina Arcani"—the precedent of the Mysteries was appealed to both by Catholics and Protestants. One of the ablest of the latter, W. E. Tentzel (*Exercitationes Selectae*, Pars ii. Lipsiae, 1692), points out that resemblances between pagan and Christian institutions naturally arose, without any ecclesiastical decree, from the previous education and habits of proselytes. Our countryman David Clarkson, on the other hand, in his *Discourse concerning Liturgies* (1689), held that the Church deliberately adopted rites resembling those of paganism, with a view of attracting those who were without. Bingham (*Antiquities*, bk. x. ch. 5) approached the subject with his usual caution and impartiality, and what he has written is still worth consulting. Mosheim (*De Rebus Christianorum ante Constant.* p. 319 *ff.* ed. 1753) is as clear and sensible on this matter as he generally is on others, differing little in substance from Casaubon, who is also followed in the main by J. A. Stark (*Tralatitia ex Gentilismo in Religionem Christianam*, Regiomont. 1774, pp. 7-17).

In our own time the consideration of the influence of the pagan Mysteries on nascent Christianity has again become prominent. R. Rothe's essay *De Disciplina Arcani* (Heidelberg, 1831) with his article on *Arcan-Disciplin* in Herzog's *Real-Encyclop.* (I. 469 *ff.* 1st ed.) threw much light on the subject. G. von Zezschwitz devoted a section of his admirable *Christl.-Kirchlich. Katechetik* (I. 154-209), and also subsequently an article in the second edition of Herzog's *Real-Encyclop.* (I. 637 *ff.*) to a careful examination of the relations between the pagan and the Christian Mysteries, whether with regard to terminology or to rites. While he sees clearly some resemblances, and even thinks that Christian forms were deliberately taken from rites already existing, he rejects emphatically the supposition that the spirit which animates Christian rites is in any way akin to that of paganism. It was through the works of Rothe and Zezschwitz that I was first attracted to the comparison of Christian and pagan Mysteries, and I have no doubt that whatever I have written bears traces of their influence, even though I have been unable to acknowledge my obligation in detail.

In our own country the influence of the Mysteries on the forms of Christian worship has been discussed with great learning and ability by the late Dr. Edwin Hatch (*Hibbert Lectures*, 1888, lect. 10). This lecture was, unfortunately, left unrevised at the time of the author's lamented death. It received the loving care of very able friends, but no such care can fully make up for the lack of the final revision of the author himself, and probably the friends of one who is departed do not feel themselves at liberty to change the author's words, even when they may think them erroneous. The lecture therefore appears under serious disadvantages, and might, perhaps, claim a certain exemption from criticism. I have, however, thought myself bound to notice it, because it is in it that the Mysteries and their influence on ecclesiastical rites have been most prominently brought before English readers.

But the most complete work on the subject before us is Gustav Anrich's *Das antike Mysterienwesen in seinem Einfluss auf das Christenthum* (Göttingen, 1894), the fulness, accuracy, and sound judgment of which leave little to be desired. I had already made some study of the subject and arrived at most of the conclusions stated in the following pages before it appeared; but I have still learned much from it, and I desire to express in the fullest manner my obligations to it, the more so as they are of a nature which can sometimes not be particularly acknowledged. The *Religionsgeschichtliche Studien zur Frage der Beeinflussung des Urchristenthums durch das antike Mysterienwesen* of Georg Wobbermin (Berlin, 1896), who controverts some of

Anrich's conclusions, I had not seen when these Lectures were written, but I have occasionally referred to him in the Notes.

In these Lectures I have not attempted to give anything like a complete account of pagan and Christian Mysteries, or of their relations to each other; my limited space forbade the attempt to treat fully so large a subject. What I have endeavoured to do is to remove what appear to me misconceptions or errors. In the first place, I wish to show that the reluctance which many excellent persons feel to believe that Christianity, as it actually exists in the world, derived anything from the paganism in the midst of which it arose is not altogether reasonable. With regard to the Mysteries in particular, I have attempted to show that Christian Churches in the midst of paganism were of necessity "Mysteries" in the old sense, as being societies formed for the sake of a worship which was neither domestic nor civic; that while they concealed, as all others concealed, their most sacred rites from the gaze of the profane, their general teaching was perfectly public and open; and that such secrecy as existed was not a later accretion, but primitive. Finally, I have criticised, I hope not unfairly, some statements of recent English writers as to the indebtedness of the Church to the ancient mystic worship. I am far from denying that such indebtedness exists, but it seems in some cases to have been pressed further than the evidence warrants.

S. CHEETHAM.

ROCHESTER, *4th September* 1897.

CONTENTS

LECTURE I

THE SEED AND ITS GROWTH

Phenomena of growth, p. 1 ; growth of individuals is a formative process, 7 ; growth of societies, including the Christian Church, is similar, 8 ; the Church's power of seizing and modifying modes of thought and action already existing, 12 ; does not annihilate character, 14 ; Christianity must use popular language with its associations, 15 ; pagan art, 19 ; forms of worship, 20 ; but some rites practised by Christians are not Christian rites, 21 ; similar forms arise from similar circumstances, 22 ; Hellenising of the Church, 24 ; Christianity not a mere natural product of forces working in the first century, 29 ; failure of pagan philosophy, 31 ; work of the Church, 32.

LECTURE II

THE RISE OF MYSTERIES

Family and civic worship in antiquity, 37 ; belief in immortality, 39 ; societies for peculiar worship, called Mysteries, 40 ; general purpose of such societies not a secret, 42 ; to what did initiation admit ? 43 ; secrecy required, 44 ; the great earth-deities, Demeter, Persephone, and Dionysus, 46 ; Orphic mysticism, 49 ; Eleusis, 50 ; Egyptian deities, Osiris, Isis, Horus, 52 ; associated with the departed, 54 ; Serapis, 55 ; Plutarch, 56 ; Apuleius, 57 ; Mithras the Sun-god, 59 ; general characteristics of Mysteries, 61 ; yearning for salvation, 63 ; difference between the secret of Mysteries and the secret of Christianity, 65.

LECTURE III

THE SECRET OF THE MYSTERIES AND OF THE CHURCH

Prevalence of Mysteries in the first century, 71; their influence on the Church, 72; the question is of things, not names, 74; use of the words φωτισμός and σφραγίς, 75; possible modification of pagan rites after the Christian era, 77; secrecy of certain rites in the Mysteries and in the Church, 78; non-Christians excluded from the Eucharist from the earliest times, 79; the general traits of Christian teaching universally known, 81; certain formulas kept secret, 82; classes of candidates for baptism, 90; instruction given from primitive times, 91; no parallel in paganism, 94.

LECTURE IV

BAPTISM AND THE HOLY EUCHARIST

Grades of pagan initiation, 99; preliminary purifications, 100; Mithraic baptism, 103; delivery of initiation, 105; the symbol or watchword, 106; use of lights, 107; chaplets, 110; supposed origin of Eucharist, 110; nothing in Eleusinian Mysteries resembled the blessing of the Bread and Wine, 112; anticipations of the Eucharistic feast in paganism, 115; diptychs, 117; general tone and influence of Mysteries, 119; pagans did not always approve of Mysteries, 122; indecent symbols, 124; conclusion, 126.

NOTES

Conception of life, 131; *Le Christianisme et ses Origines*, 131; Characteristics of Gnostic teachers, 133; terms used to designate Mysteries, 135; φωτισμός and σφραγίς, 143; Mithraic grades, 145; cyceon and the contents of the mystic chest, 147; supposed sacrifice of a lamb, 149.

LECTURE I

I

"The kingdom of heaven is like to a grain of mustard seed, which a man took, and sowed in his field."—St. Matthew xiii. 31.

THE little seed which we cast into the earth contains within itself some power or property which man could not give, and which we call life.[1] When it is placed in a proper matrix, it draws into itself that which it needs from the earth, the rain, the air, and the sun, and becomes a plant, perhaps a great tree, in which the birds of the air may make their dwellings. All the elements of which the tree is formed were in existence from the creation of the world, for in the physical universe nothing perishes, but without the germ of life contained in the seed they would never have coalesced into the special organism which we call a tree. Each tree is a unique production. It does not exactly resemble any other tree, even of the same species, but is modified in a thousand ways by the circumstances under which it lives and grows. The cells and cell walls are formed from matter previously existing, which may already have formed part of other organisms, and is destined again to be resolved. But the process of growth is not at all less wonderful because the result of growth is composed of certain elements well known to us. If the same elements were again put together by a chemist they would not form a tree. They would lack life. When the tree dies, we "know not where is that Promethean heat" which can its life restore. The maxim "omne vivum ex vivo" still remains unshaken.

Again, we may be sure that a skilful woodman will plant a tree at the season and in the soil which are most likely to foster its growth. He will not plant an elm in the crag where only a pine can cling, nor an oak in the soil where only a beech will flourish. He will give to each tree its own nurture.

And there is yet another phenomenon of growth which it is well to notice. When many trees are planted in a limited space, it is the strongest sapling which rises towards heaven and spreads its branches over the earth. The surrounding shoots, which started with it in the race of life, are dwarfed or even killed by their more vigorous brother; they fail to gain the light and air which are necessary to their subsistence. And the decay of the brushwood beneath a spreading and towering tree goes to form a better soil to aid the growth of the greater one. To the one that hath, more is given.

Further, the early stages of this wondrous growth are the most obscure, the least explicable.

> When Nature tries her finest touch,
>   Weaving her vernal wreath,
> Mark ye how close she veils her round,
> Not to be traced by sight or sound
>   Nor soiled by ruder breath?

The words of the poet are true. However accurately we may observe the conditions which are necessary for the development of a particular seed, the power which actually causes growth remains a mystery. The fresh green of spring-time is a perpetual wonder.

Doubtless the processes of growth are what we call natural; they take place in accordance with what we call laws of nature. But there is no real opposition between God and nature, between that which is natural and that which is divine. We apply the word "natural" to the series of phenomena which take place in that portion of the universe in which we have been able to trace invariable sequences; but the cause of all these phenomena is the will of God, which is the cause of all things; of the things which occur in unvarying sequence, as well as of those the laws of which we have not been able to trace. And man is himself, in a sense, a part of nature. For him also, in this world, there is birth, decay, and death. His families and tribes, his nations and states, are formed under the pressure of laws from which he cannot withdraw himself. We express a truth when we speak of the laws of human nature. Capricious as the impulses of individual men may seem, they are yet restrained within certain limits, and we see in history that every nation of men works with wonderful steadiness, however unconsciously, towards certain ends. It is something more than a metaphor when we speak of a state as an organism, a body having a life of its own, a body capable of growth and dissolution.

Now, when the Lord likens the kingdom of heaven to a seed cast into the ground, He teaches us first of all that the Church of Christ on earth is a growth; it is an organism, not a finished structure. It did not come on earth, like the new Jerusalem of the seer's vision, complete and four-square in all its parts, everywhere flooded with the glory of God; it began with a seed cast upon the earth. The seed is the Word of God; not merely the spoken message of the kingdom, but the Son of God Himself, the Incarnate Word, in whose life the Church lives. And except the seed "fall into the ground and die, it abideth by itself alone; but if it die it beareth much fruit." Life rises from apparent death.

And growth is a process which is not creative, in the sense of bringing new matter into existence, but formative. That which is peculiar to each plant is the mysterious power which gives to each seed its own body, a power which no analysis can reach. And something of the same kind seems to be found in societies. All societies are of course formed of men, men of the same flesh and blood, the same nerves and brains—differing, indeed, widely in some respects, but all showing the great traits of our common nature. With whatever superficial differences, men are everywhere men. And over the communities of mankind a power presides of which they are unconscious, causing them to assume their varied forms, forms changing from age to age, growing, decaying, dying. However the spirit which animates one nation may differ from that which gives life to another, all alike are formed from the constant elements of the same humanity.

And the great divine society, the Church of Christ, is, as regards its outward form, no exception to this. Its origin, indeed, admits of no comparison at all with that of any other society; the seed from which it sprang is divine in a sense absolutely unique and unparalleled; the spirit which animates and guides it differs altogether in kind from that which moves any other community; yet is it formed of the same elements as any other, and grows under similar laws. The gray lichen on the wall and the most gorgeous product of tropical vegetation are composed of the same protoplasm, and are subject to the same laws of growth, though their forms are so widely different. The Church of Christ had impressed upon it by its Founder a certain form or idea from which it cannot deviate, any more than the pine can clothe itself in the foliage of the oak; yet, while preserving its essential form, it is in many ways modified from age to age. It does not annihilate all previously existing forms of thought or all previously existing institutions; rather, it imbues them with its own spirit and adapts them to its own purposes.

The early Christian apologists would probably have had no difficulty in admitting that the Church was influenced by the philosophies and the institutions which it found existing. This was not, indeed, the problem which they treated, but in defending themselves against the charge of innovation they recognised in the frankest manner the presence of the Word of God in the nations of the earth, their philosophies and their moral precepts. For them the Gospel of Christ existed at least in germ in the days of Abraham and of Moses, nay, from the beginning of the world;[2] to them God in Christ was the source of all good, at all times and in all places. The same Word which wrought in Hebrew prophets produced also the truthfulness, righteousness, and nobleness which were found among the Gentiles; all who lived in accordance with right reason were, so far, Christians, even though, like Socrates, they were thought to deny their country's gods. The great achievements of lawgivers and philosophers were not without the Word, however imperfectly apprehended. Even to Tertullian, the many phrases in which heathens expressed their recognition of one God over all were "the utterances of a soul naturally Christian"; and we can imagine that if Justin, or Clement, or Origen had seen such a collection of Christian sentiments before Christ as that which in our days has been made by Ernest Havet,[3] he would have rejoiced to see so conspicuous an exhibition of the power of the Word. But he would by no means have admitted that these scattered sayings, however excellent, were the origins of Christianity. The origin of Christianity, he would have said, is He who founded the great society by and through which these excellent sentiments were made living and growing truths. Early Christian writers abundantly recognise the presence of the Word everywhere, and therefore could hardly have been shocked if it had been pointed out to them that many of their own precepts and customs were older than Christianity. Even St. Augustine, though he once spoke of the virtues of the heathen as splendid sins, in the calmer mood of later life declared that the very thing which is now called the Christian religion was found among the ancients, even from the creation of mankind, though it was not until Christ came in the flesh that the true religion, which already existed, came to be called Christian.[3] In later times a generation arose which would hardly admit any direct operation of the Spirit since the days of the Apostles, and to this generation it was a shock to be told by Tindal, almost in the words of St. Augustine, that Christianity was as old as the creation.

And it is indeed impossible to conceive the kingdom of God rising and growing in any other way than by seizing and modifying the modes of thought and action with which it has been brought into contact. For there is no starting afresh, clear of all prejudices and prepossessions, in the life of man. There is never any epoch in which all questions are open. No atom of the human race can stand alone; God has willed that man should have a home and a country; that parents and schoolmasters, laws and customs, should play an immense part in moulding his being. This is a fact which no one denies. Even those who contend that the mind of a new-born infant is a clear tablet, still admit that it is scribbled over with strange and varied forms long before he consciously encounters the great problems which perplex man from age to age. We are all influenced by the associations of our earliest years—associations often bound by subtle ties with generations long gone by. To every one of us there comes a birthright of traditional influences which forms the first provision for our journey in the world. And this great body of unwritten tradition is continually changed and superseded by the thoughts and feelings which a new age brings forth around us. Sometimes this change is so slow that the thoughts of the son scarcely differ from those of the father; sometimes so rapid that between succeeding generations there is a great gulf fixed, across which the new looks with scorn on the old, the old with sorrow and bitterness on the new. As in the growing tree old leaves fall and are replaced by new, so in every healthy society old opinions become obsolete and new are formed. Change is necessary for the life of a society as well as of a plant or an animal; but it is well to remember the caution of one of "the first of those that know," Francis Bacon[1]: "It were good that men in their innovations would follow the example of Time itself, which indeed innovated greatly, but quietly, and by degrees scarce to be perceived."

We see then working in human life, on the

one side use and wont, custom, habit, which render society possible; on the other, constant change, rejection of that which is worn-out and useless, adoption of that which is fresh and new; but the new things always grow out of the old; there is never a fresh start independent of that which went before. Probably no body of men ever made a more vigorous effort to make all things new, to remodel everything on certain principles without the smallest respect for tradition, than the leaders of the French Revolution at the end of the last century, and yet we know that relics of the Old Régime were everywhere built into the structure of the new constitution.[5]

When a new society arises, it must in the first instance be composed of full-grown men, who have their senses exercised to discern good and evil. And these full-grown men will be already imbued with the thoughts, feelings, and habits of their own age. Doubtless the change wrought in the hearts of men, the transformation of character, by the Holy Spirit, is immense. He that sitteth on the throne saith, "Behold, I make all things new." They are no vain words when the Apostle tells us, that "if any man be in Christ, he is a new creature; the old things have passed away, behold they have become new." Yet is this great change not so complete and thorough but that old characteristics remain. St. Paul and St. John were both moved by the Holy Spirit, but it cannot be said that their minds have taken the same mould; Clement and Origen, Tertullian and Cyprian, all served the same Lord, all received the same Spirit, all cherished the same hope, and yet the mind trained in Alexandrian philosophy apprehends the message in a very different way from that in which it is received by a mind formed in African schools of rhetoric and courts of law.

It is very obvious, though it seems sometimes to have been forgotten, that the Church of necessity adopted at any rate the language of those to whom it brought its message. The first preachers of the Gospel must use words familiar to those whom they addressed. In order to be "understanded of the people" they must use popular language, and the New Testament is a witness that they did so. They spoke the Greek language which they heard around them, as we find it preserved in the works of the philosophers, historians, and comedians both of their own time and of that which went before.[6] The list of words which, before the apostolic writings, are found in the Septuagint only is but a short one, and does not include many of the most characteristic terms of Christianity. Now words are stamped with the philosophies, the religions, the superstitions, and the customs of those through whose mouths they have passed. But a word may be, and most words are, so worn by use that the original image and superscription are no longer visible except to skilled investigators; they pass current without a thought of the mint whence they were issued. Their present value in mental commerce is the only thing considered. This is so obvious that I should scarcely think it necessary to mention it were it not that it seems to have been ignored by some earnest and able inquirers. We shall have occasion to notice presently how often the assumption has been made that when the early Christians adopted a word they must needs have adopted also the philosophy or the ceremony which the word was originally employed to designate. And yet no assumption could be more fallacious. That Christians adopted from the first many expressions derived from pagan philosophy or pagan ceremonies is certain, but in considering these it is well to bear in mind the words of one of the ablest investigators of pagan religion under the Empire, Gaston Boissier[7]: "When the Church formed its language it did, no doubt, create many new expressions, but it also adopted many which seemed made for it by the philosophers of the time. In reality all these verbal resemblances are of little importance. Similarities of idea appear at first more serious, but they are often only apparent, and a more careful examination will show that at the bottom there is never a complete agreement between the two doctrines." What Boissier says of the terms which Christianity borrowed from pagan philosophy is, I believe, quite as true of those which it borrowed from pagan religion.

Christians of the first days had no scruple whatever in adopting words which had been used in the service of paganism. Take one of the most sacred of Christian terms, Σωτήρ, Saviour. This was not only in common use among pagans, but it was distinctly associated with pagan worship. It was a constant epithet of Zeus and other tutelary deities; in ancient Greece perhaps hardly a banquet was held in which the name of Zeus the saviour was not invoked over the third goblet; it had been the distinctive name of more than one Egyptian king; grateful cities added the title "Saviour" to the name of an emperor who had done them some service.[8] None the less did Christians avail themselves of the word to designate the true Saviour of the world; and it would be mere folly to suppose that in using the word they transferred to the divine Son the attributes of a pagan deity or a pagan sovereign. Christians early adopted the pagan names of the days of the week, which we retain in a Teutonic form even to this day; but who supposes that in appropriating these they adopted also the Chaldean astrology from which they are derived? They no more scrupled to call a day Mercury's or Saturn's than to speak of a man as Apollos or Artemas. Who, when he uses the word "January," thinks of the old Italian deity from whom the name is derived, or, when he mentions February, of the great festival of expiation among the Romans? "Verba notionum tesserae," said Bacon; words are counters for mental conceptions; what their connotation is must be ascertained by other considerations than those of mere etymology or original usage. A word in its time plays many parts, and it is not always easy to ascertain what it represents in a particular instance. There is, perhaps, no department of Christian archæology in which verbal fallacies have been more frequent than in the discussion of the relation between the Mysteries of paganism and the Mysteries of the Christian Church.

And Christianity adopted to a large extent pagan art. So far as regards style and manner of treatment this was, in fact, matter of necessity, for when a Christian of the earliest age wished to place some memorial of a friend departed, or to decorate a place of worship, he could find no workmen but such as had been trained in pagan schools. But the adoption of pagan art went beyond this. In the ancient Church the figure of the Good Shepherd occupied much the same place which in the Middle Ages was taken by the crucifix. The resemblance of the shepherd bearing a lamb to the Hermes Criophoros of the pagans has often been noticed, and is, I believe, scarcely denied. The fabled Orpheus became in the declining days of paganism the centre of a mystic system of teaching and worship; yet this did not prevent the early Church from seizing the all-wise, all-attractive singer and teacher as a type of the Lord Himself. And so in many other instances.

And there can be little doubt that the forms of Christian worship were in some degree influenced by the forms already existing when Christ was first preached. A pagan who had been accustomed all his life to kneel in prayer, or to stand with expanded arms in the temple of his deity, would probably continue to do so when he had learned to worship God in Christ. So long as the accustomed forms were in themselves innocent, what need to deviate from them? That much passed over in this way from paganism to Christianity can scarcely be doubted; and as it has come to be alleged of late years that the pagan Mysteries contributed much, not only to the outward form of Christian worship, but even to its conception, it seems worth while to attempt to examine how far this allegation is true. To this, therefore, I propose to devote the remaining lectures of this course. But before proceeding to details there are still a few general principles to which I desire to direct attention.

When we come to speak of the adoption by the Church of institutions, customs, or rites which already existed in paganism, we must bear in mind that rites which Christians practise are not necessarily Christian rites. Even to this day, for instance, rites are practised in the harvest-field in almost every part of Europe which can be traced to an age long before Christianity.[9] But no canon of the Church sanctions them; on the contrary the ceremonies of the Rogation Days, when the blessing of God is asked on the growing corn, were probably intended to supersede them. The popular observances of May-day and Christmas are vastly more ancient than the ecclesiastical services of those days. They are neither Christian nor un-Christian, but simply a part of our inheritance as children of the great Aryan race. Our forefathers continued practices to which they had grown accustomed, regarding them as innocent in themselves and compatible with their Christian profession. When such rites were adopted by Christian people they had probably already lost their original significance.

Again, when an institution arises naturally from the circumstances of the society in which it exists, there is no need to suppose that it is derived from a similar custom in another society where it arose equally naturally. For instance, there is no need to derive the Christian sermon or homily from the harangues of the sophists; for wherever there are assemblies of men there is oratory, and the style of this oratory is determined by the culture and mental attitude of the speaker and the hearers; the spiritual force and spontaneity of such addresses vary with the preacher. It does so now, and doubtless has done so in all ages of the Church. There is no generic difference between "prophesying" and "preaching." An oration of St. John Chrysostom is much more elaborate than the homily which we call the Second Epistle of Clement, but are we to say that it is on that account less spiritual? Who would deny the gifts of the Spirit to one who, in spite of the shrinking of a sensitive nature, could boldly rebuke vice and patiently suffer for the truth as Chrysostom did?

Again, we need not shrink from admitting that in the form of their election of Church officers the early Christians may have been influenced by the methods of election which they saw everywhere in the Empire. But there is no need to suppose deliberate imitation; to do so is to frame a gratuitous hypothesis. For their forms were such as, under whatever names, are common to all elections. At every election some one must preside, who must receive nominations of candidates and the votes of the electors; some one must declare upon whom the choice of the electors has fallen; and if the president is not himself the person who can admit to office him who has been chosen, he must return the names of the elected to the person or the body which has that power. This was the course of proceeding in civil and also in ecclesiastical elections, but it is not necessary to suppose that the latter was an imitation of the former, because from the nature of things an election could hardly take place in any other way.

And as to the Hellenising of the Church during the first three centuries. During that period the whole educated world within the Empire was Hellenised, and as the Church drew into itself larger numbers of the cultured class, it shared more and more in Hellenic culture. The form of its literature and its theology was changed. It could not withdraw itself from that which we have grown accustomed to call the Zeit-geist or Time-spirit. But that it received a specially Hellenic tinge from the grandiose follies of Gnosticism it is difficult to believe.[10] If the Greek genius is such as a master of the subject[11] has painted it; if it loved, as he assures us that it did, "to see things as they really are, to discern their meanings and adjust their relations"; if it followed boldly in the way where reason led;—

then is Gnosticism, propounding explanations of the phenomena of the universe which rest entirely on authority unsupported by reason, wide as the poles asunder from Hellenism. It belongs to the speculations of those Eastern nations which—again to quote Professor Butcher—"loved to move in a region of twilight, content with that half-knowledge which stimulates the religious sense." That Gnosticism exercised a great influence on the development of the early Church no one who has studied the subject will deny, but that influence can scarcely have been directly in favour of Hellenism. It would probably be truer to say that Greek dialectic was developed within the Church in opposition to the Oriental figments of the Gnostic teachers. The early defenders of the Church were perfectly confident that right reason was on their side, and they used it to destroy the gorgeous illusions of their opponents. This contest very largely influenced the development of Christian theology. But even without it, we can hardly doubt that a theology would have been evolved not materially different from that which actually arose. Some kind of theology there needs must be. A system which claims to deal authoritatively with man's destiny and his relation to the Deity must have some struggle with systems of philosophy which attempt the same task; and such a contest must be fought on common ground and with the same kind of weapons. The methods of the rabbis would be ineffectual against men trained in Athenian schools. And further, it is scarcely possible for a man to receive momentous truths into his mind without some attempt to give reasons for them, to systematise them, to allot them their place in the general history of human thought. These natural instincts, working upon the solemn and all-important subject-matter, the Incarnation of the Son of God for the redemption and renewal of man, produced Christian theology; and as the culture of the whole educated class of the Empire in the early ages of Christianity was, directly or indirectly, Hellenic, it took of necessity Hellenic forms. It would have been strange, indeed, if those who wrought at the great structure of Christian theology had stood within a charmed circle into which no breath of the time-spirit could penetrate. There was in fact no such seclusion.

We are thankful to know that the work of the Holy Spirit is not limited to the Christian Church; Gentiles also have uttered words in accordance with the mind of Christ,—Gentiles also have earnestly contended for righteousness and self-control, even when they doubted of judgment to come. No inquiry is more momentous and more interesting than that which attempts to search out and discriminate the influences which have made Christianity what it is. Such questions as these—What ground was provided for Christianity? What already existing views and teachings could it draw into itself, purify and glorify? What circumstances prepared the way for it, facilitated and furthered its extension? How did paganism react upon Christianity?—require an answer. And if we have to say, that the circumstances of the time were very favourable to the spread of Christianity in the first ages of its existence; that pagan training and pagan customs did exert considerable influence on the outward form of the kingdom of God on earth, our faith in its divine origin is in no way shaken. We do but the more venerate the wisdom and power of the Almighty God who so ruled what we call the natural course of this world that it furthered the growth of His spiritual kingdom.

The Church of Christ has, in fact, shown a wonderful power of absorbing and assimilating thoughts and institutions already existing in the world. But there is, of course, a limit to this process; it cannot adopt everything that it finds. For instance, the Eucharistic feast at Corinth described by St. Paul, probably differed little in outward form from the ἔρανος, the common meal of a pagan society to which each member brought a contribution. There was no reason why such a festival should not be Christianised; it contained nothing in its nature profane or un-Christian. But it was impossible for a Christian to take part in a sacrificial feast in honour of the fancied supernatural beings of heathendom; this would have been a breach of his allegiance to Christ. It was, to say the least, inexpedient for a Christian knowingly to eat meat which had formed part of a victim, even though it was sold in the public shambles, and was commonly partaken of without a thought of the purpose which it had served. Some rites were too deeply tainted with paganism to be adopted into the service of Christianity.

We are sometimes assured that Christianity itself is a mere natural product of various moral and intellectual forces working in the Empire, more particularly from the time of Augustus to that of Marcus Aurelius. Now, suppose we grant that many fragments of the Sermon on the Mount are to be found in the Manual of Epictetus or the Thoughts of Marcus Aurelius, the fact has still to be explained, that neither Epictetus nor even Marcus Aurelius, armed as he was with supreme power, has done more than provide edifying and interesting books for a few students, while Christ and His disciples, starting on their course in poverty and weakness, from an obscure corner, have in fact conquered the most powerful, the most productive, the most progressive races of the world. This is a fact of which historical science requires an explanation. We need not hesitate to admit that the growth of the Christian Church was promoted by the state of society in which it first appeared; the Lord of the universe caused the seed to be sown in soil prepared for it. How could it be otherwise? So far as we are able to judge, the faith would have spread less rapidly in the republican days when political life absorbed all the thoughts of a free citizen than it did in the time when those "obstinate questionings of sense and outward things," those "blank misgivings of a creature moving about in worlds not realised" asserted themselves, and men wandered in the mazes of painful thought. This we may admit; but this is a very different thing from saying that the forces working in society produced Christianity. The fact is that the characteristic teaching of Christianity was something of which paganism knew nothing, and which it could hardly comprehend.

St. Paul, we know, did not think of the heathen as without God; but in his epistles how much do we find that could by any possibility have been drawn from ethnic sources? Some moral precepts we may find identical with some in Seneca or in other Stoical writings, but the root of the matter, the being "in Christ," is altogether unknown in paganism. In truth, when Christ came the mind of weary paganism seemed to be worn out. A last desperate attempt to reach the alienated divine life was made by Neo-Platonism;[12] it failed, and ancient philosophy sank into complete exhaustion. Nothing fresh and original was produced until European thought had been thoroughly leavened by Christianity. Christianity, far from crushing philosophy, gave it a new life. We may perhaps illustrate what took place in the world by the history of a single soul. When St. Augustine was an ardent youth of nineteen the reading of Cicero's *Hortensius* made him conscious of the seriousness of life, and of the folly and vanity of the course which he was pursuing; but it was not until he read, in deep emotion and after long struggles, the words in which St. Paul bids us put on the Lord Jesus Christ, that the clouds were dispersed and the true light shone into his soul. So in the world at large, the old religions and philosophies had opened the eyes of many a soul to see how vain and unsatisfying was the pursuit of mere pleasure and amusement, wealth and power; but Christ alone could teach them that knowledge of God which is eternal life, and so give them rest and peace.

And what explanation is there of the growth, the assimilating power of the Church of Christ, except that it has a gift from on high, something which man could not give, which enables it to draw into its wondrous organisation the moral and spiritual good things which are already extant in the world,—a ferment, working so as to make from poor and feeble elements a mass heaving with spiritual life, containing the true food of the human soul? And the great tree of the Lord's planting has brought forth much fruit from age to age. True, the life of the Church is not yet pure and perfect; the tree produces not only good fruit, meet for the Master of the garden when He cometh seeking it, but withered and cankered growths, fit only to be again resolved with a view to new life; it needs constantly the stern yet merciful hand of the keeper of the ground to clear away the evil for the sake of the good. Yet, with whatever shortcomings, the tree lives and grows and bears much fruit. Unfold the long record of the lives and acts of those who have served Christ. Even in those whom we agree to call in a special sense " saints " we find errors, and even what the world calls follies; but with all this, how much pure aspiration after the heavenly life, how much self-sacrifice, how much devotion to the good of others, how much eagerness to serve the Lord who redeemed and sanctified them! And not only do we find such traits as these in the many volumes which record achievements such as the world would not willingly let die, but everywhere and in every age there have been thousands and millions of hidden saints whose names are written in the Book of Life. A man must have been very unfortunate if in the course of his days he has not met some in whom he could trace the lineaments of Christ — something of the sweetness, gentleness, unselfishness, and devotion to the service of the Father of which the Great Exemplar is the Lord Himself. While these are plainly seen we need not fear lest the Church of Christ should become wholly worldly and pagan. Such light as this is not overcome of darkness, such life as this is not conquered by death.

LECTURE II

II

> "And yet God left not himself without witness, in that he did good, and gave you from heaven rains and fruitful seasons, filling your hearts with food and gladness."—ACTS xiv. 17.

THESE words, in which St. Paul points to man's constant recognition of supernatural powers, causing the growth of the corn and the fruits by which he is fed, may well introduce the consideration of the question, What association of thought induced primitive man to ascribe to the deities of vegetation the care of the souls of the dead?

Our classical studies have probably made us more familiar with pagan mythology than with pagan worship, and yet worship played a part in the ancient pagan city even greater, probably, than it did in a city of the Middle Ages. Every family, every city had its own gods, its own ritual. But the worship paid to these gods was not what we understand by religion. It did not attempt to open to the eager spirit "a road to bring us daily nearer God." It was merely a curious medley of traditional rites and practices, the real meaning of which had often been lost. When we use the word "religion" we think of a creed, of definite teaching about God and man, and the relations of man to God; of solemn services, in which we join with heart and mind, knowing whom we worship. The civic and family worship of the classic pagans implied none of these things. It was only the ceremonies which were regarded as important; to observe them was an imperious necessity, for without them the family or the State could not flourish. Certain formal observances were due to the ancestors of a family, to the gods and heroes of a State; these must be paid, not only from a feeling of duty and reverence, but to render the objects of worship friendly and helpful. As Marquardt says, nothing could be less like a Christian Church than a pagan temple.[13]

But family and civic worship was by no means the whole of ancient religion. In the ancient as in the modern world man felt the need of some explanation of the wonders and perplexities in the midst of which he found himself. To explain these was the task of philosophy; but the teachings of philosophy were of necessity accessible only to an audience which, however fit, was few. There were thoughts in the unlettered also which were not satisfied by the traditional forms of the family and the State. There was the inextinguishable need for something to rouse the soul to an ecstasy of religious emotion such as the ordinary ceremony, public or domestic, did not produce. In particular, if we look back on the traditions of the great Aryan race to which we belong, we find that our forefathers never regarded the few years which we pass on earth as the whole of life. Long before the rise of philosophy men believed in some kind of renewed existence after death.[14] And if something of the sentient being survived, it was inevitable to ask,

> What worlds or what vast regions hold
> The unbodied soul that hath forsook
> Her mansion in this fleshly nook?

Do all endure the same fate, or are there

distinctions of weal and woe in the unseen world? If so, can man do anything to secure a portion among the blessed? Can he help to bless his brethren who have departed? Are there lustral waters, are there charms and soothing words which can purify the soul and render it fit to bear company with those whom the gods love? Such thoughts as these gave rise to a multitude of societies which attempted to satisfy man's need of religious emotion, together with his longing for a feeling of brotherhood in religion, and to give him hope of a state of bliss after his departure from the earthly life. These societies may conveniently be designated Mysteries.[15] But when we use this word we must guard ourselves from the associations which in the course of two thousand years have gathered round it. The word Mystery was the name of a religious society founded, not on citizenship or on kindred, but on the choice of its members, for the practice of rites by which, it was believed, their happiness might be promoted both in this world and in the next. The Greek word μυστήριον does not, of its own force, imply anything, in our sense of the word, mysterious, that is to say, obscure or difficult to comprehend. That which it connotes is rather something which can only be known on being imparted by some one already in possession of it, not by mere reason and research which are common to all. It may be, in itself, of the simplest nature. In fact, from the nature of the case, the special disclosure made in a Mystery must have been of such a nature that an ordinary man could understand it, or at least suppose himself to understand. It was for ordinary intelligences that Mysteries were formed. Lobeck[16] defines Mysteries as "those sacred rites which took place, not in the sight of all or in the full light of day and at public altars, but either in the night, or within closed sanctuaries, or in remote and solitary places." And he divides them into three classes. First, civic Mysteries, such as the Eleusinian at Athens, which were in the charge of public officials; second, fanatical rites, like those of the Great Mother and of Bacchus, whether such as were recognised by the State, or private celebrations such as those of the Orphic votaries; third, occasional functions performed on behalf of private persons for the purpose of appeasing the manes or of averting evil. This seems a fair division, except that we must bear in mind that Lobeck's second class includes rites to which we should scarcely apply the epithet fanatical. The worship of Isis or of Mithras have scarcely anything in common with the noisy dance of the Curetes or the "riot of the tipsy Bacchanals."

The great purpose of the mystic rites seems to have been known to others beside the initiated.[17] Those who presented themselves for initiation knew of what kind was the illumination which they were to look for. The teaching of those in Eleusis, for instance, as to the greater blessedness of the initiated in the under-world, was known to all Athens; it excited the imagination of the graver poets, and was brought on the stage by comedians. Still, none but the initiated, the instructed, could be present at the services, just as in the ordinary national processions and sacrifices none but members of the nation could take part. The great question is, to what did initiation admit? Aristotle[18] assures us that what men gained in the Mysteries was not definite instruction, but impressions and emotions. This is said of the Eleusinian Mysteries, but it probably applies more or less to all. And we know that the culminating point of initiation was admission to a spectacle in which, amid a blaze of light, were probably exhibited, together with the histories of certain gods, the horrors which awaited the wicked, and the blessedness of the pious in the Elysian fields.[19] The rewards and punishments of a future state were not first revealed to the initiated when they entered the sacred hall, but they received a new vividness and caused a fresh emotion. The feelings of the newly-admitted votary may have been, in fact, not very unlike those of one who, already acquainted with the general teaching of the Christian faith, is brought into a stately church where sights and sounds combine to surround old truths with a halo of sanctity and majesty which the bare recital of them could not give.[20] If this is the true conception, that which was imparted to the candidate for initiation, as a preliminary to the spectacle, can hardly have been more than the exhibition of sacred objects,[21] with perhaps some directions for his conduct in the yet unknown chamber, and for some responses which he was to make in the service.

It is even uncertain whether the address of the hierophant contained any injunction of secrecy. The herald's proclamation for silence almost certainly refers rather to the awful silence to be observed during the celebration than to any reserve practised by the worshippers. Pausanias, in the second century A.D.,[22] feared to reveal what he had learned within the Eleusinian temple. "What took place within the temple," he says, "the dream forbade me to write, and in any case it is unbecoming for the uninitiated even to inquire about things from the sight of which they are restrained." The ground of his reticence is not anything which he heard in the temple, but a dream, and the natural shrinking which a man feels from disclosing to unsympathetic inquirers matters for which he himself feels awe and reverence. Only an ill-bred person would trouble the initiated with inquiries on so delicate a matter. Worship in ancient times seems, in fact, to have been so universally regarded as the privilege of a special body of worshippers that these were generally reluctant to reveal the details of it to those who were without. Nevertheless it seems probable that the mysteries which overspread the Empire in its later days much more resembled secret societies than the comparatively open rites of Eleusis did.

It is not necessary for our purpose to notice the forms of worship—if we may call them by that name—which were mainly orgiastic; the end of which was rather to produce violent excitement than to impart knowledge or to elevate the soul. It is only with the graver Mysteries, in which the fate of the disembodied soul was the main object of contemplation, that the ceremonies of the Christian Church can possibly be compared; and of these only those which flourished in the Empire at the time of the first preaching of Christianity immediately concern us.

A response to their anxious questions as to the destiny of the soul men sought especially in the worship of the deities who were thought to give life to the plants and trees, and of the sun who every day, with his victorious beams, drives out the darkness.

As man gazed about him in the universe, the movements of the sun, and the moon, and the stars always attracted his awe-struck wonder; and not less the phenomena of birth and growth, decay and death. With an apparently inexhaustible fecundity, the generations of plants and animals succeed each other on the surface of the earth and to the earth return. Even man himself was vaguely thought of in primitive times as having sprung originally from the earth into which his bodily frame was in the end resolved. In an age when the general conception of nature had not been formed, men referred what we should call natural phenomena to the only source of power and guidance which they could conceive, beings of the same kind as themselves, but of higher and greater faculties. Every natural process had its appropriate deity. There appears almost everywhere among men at a certain stage of culture the worship of tree-spirits and corn-spirits,[23] conceived either as existing in vegetation, or at any rate imparting to it the force by which it grows. The earth subjugated, ploughed, and sown by the hand of man, is typified in the myth of the two great goddesses, Demeter and Persephone,[24] the holy and awful queens. Demeter[25] is especially Θεσμοφόρος, the goddess of law and order; not only of the regular course of culture which brings the harvest year by year, but of the settled, orderly life of the family and the community. Persephone is the child and indispensable companion of Demeter, who, when she is lost, seeks her sorrowing, as Aphrodite seeks her Adonis, and Isis her Osiris. For the winter season she has to endure the loss of her daughter, only to find her again in spring, when the fields are green with the fresh young blades, and varied with the bright petals of the flowers. But Demeter and Persephone were not only corn-spirits; they became also, in an age beyond record, deities of the lower world, ruling over the shades of the dead.

And again Dionysus was worshipped as the power which causes the sap to rise in the trees, so that they put forth leaves and blossoms and fruit. The vine with its clusters of grapes, whence springs the wine that maketh glad the heart of man, was his greatest but by no means his only work. No worship represents in so lively traits as that of Dionysus the pantheism and hylozoism of primitive peoples; no worship gave rise to so rich a growth of imagery and symbolism. As the god of the fruit-tree and the vine, which indicate that man has risen above barbarism, he is a kindly and gentle deity, ennobling man and man's life, delighting in peace and plenty, bestowing wealth on his worshippers. Spring-time and vintage were naturally the periods of his triumph, when his praises were sung with eager exultation on the hills and in the valleys of a sunny clime. From such festivals, in the bright air of Attica, sprang not only the dithyrambus, but the gorgeous tragedy and frolic comedy which have delighted the world for more than two thousand years. As a deity of ordered cultivation, he stands opposed to the rude chaotic powers of wild nature. In winter, when the trees are bare and no fruit hangs on the bough, these anarchic forces seemed to have gained the victory. Dionysus is storm-beaten, torn, and tortured; but if he flies from his enemies, he rises again to new life and activity. Festivals to celebrate his resurrection were held by women, among the mountains, in the night, every third year about the time when the sun turns again towards the northern fields. And he belongs to the world below as well as to the world above. Under the name of Iacchos, the brother or the bridegroom of Persephone, he had his part with her and Demeter in the secret rites of Eleusis. It was this Dionysus, the deity suffering and transformed, at once evanescent and everlasting, dying and springing again to life, that was the chief divinity of the poets and mystagogues of the sect called Orphic, in whose Mysteries the soul and its fortunes when it is released from the bands of clay become the prominent and characteristic objects. The aim and end of its initiations is to procure for the soul entrance into everlasting bliss, to prevent it from re-entering into the never-ending series of forms of earthly life to which it might otherwise be destined. There is a striking resemblance in this point between the doctrines of the Orphic teachers and the Indian. Brahmins and Buddhists alike believe that man is destined to undergo a series of births in new forms, unless by asceticism and self-renunciation he escapes from the cycle.

Demeter, Persephone, and Dionysus were worshipped in the famous Mysteries which take their name from the little town of Eleusis.

These Mysteries were, however, at Athens, not merely the concern of a private society of votaries, but were what we may fairly call civic. They were, like other religious solemnities, under the charge of the king-archon, and the great temple at Eleusis (ἀνάκτορον or τελεστήριον) in which they were celebrated belonged to the State. Almost the whole population of Athens appears to have been initiated, for initiation, not birth, was still the qualification for admission. And the publicity with which portions of the rite were celebrated, with the watchfulness of the State over them, preserved these solemnities in at least comparative purity. We do not find that they were charged, as many others were, with promoting immorality. The rites of Eleusis seem to have constituted the most vital portion of Attic religion, and always to have retained something of awe and solemnity. Originally a purely local cult, they spread to the Greek colonies in Asia as part of the constitution of the daughter states, where they seem to have exercised a considerable influence both on the populace and on the philosophers. They reached Alexandria, the great mixing-bowl of East and West, in the later days of the Ptolemies; they were known at Rome in the days of Ovid, and legalised under Claudius. They were thus known and potent in the great centres of the ancient world, while they continued to flourish in their ancient home. It was not until the fourth century that the temple at Eleusis was destroyed by the Goths at the instigation of the monks who followed the hosts of Alaric."[26]

Such were the cults of the earth-deities which, whatever their origin, are most familiar to us in the forms which they assumed among the Hellenic peoples. But the deities of the ancient land of mystery, Egypt, made widespread conquests in the Empire at the expense of the old Greek and Roman divinities.[27] Even at an earlier day Greece itself had gone to school in Egypt, and to the wearied and perplexed subjects of the Empire the Egyptian teaching, with its claim to primeval antiquity and inspired wisdom, came with a solemnity and authority which was altogether lacking in the popular mythology.

It is not easy to decipher, under the accretions of later ages, the original significance of the great Egyptian triad, Osiris, Isis, Horus.[28] Yet it is tolerably clear that in them also are represented the constant dissolution and re-organisation which go on for ever in nature. Set, the destructive principle, tears to pieces the body of Osiris and scatters the fragments over the earth. Isis, at once sister and wife of the victim, gathers them together and restores them to life. From Isis and Osiris springs the child Horus. Thus the myth appears to represent the perpetual decay and growth, life and death, which are everywhere present in the world. The ears of corn with which the Isis-statues of the Roman period are often crowned are probably a reminiscence of the early character of the goddess as presiding over the springing of the fresh corn. And the character of Osiris[29] as a god of vegetation is shown in the legend that he taught men the use of corn and the cultivation of the grape, and by the fact that his annual festival began with a solemn ploughing of the earth. In the temple of Isis at Philæ the dead body of Osiris is represented with stalks of corn springing from it, which a priest waters from a vessel which he holds in his hand. An inscription sets forth that "this is the form of him whom we may not name, Osiris of the Mysteries, who sprang from the returning waters." Clearly he was a personification of the corn which sprang from the yearly watered valley. And a later process in the treatment of the corn, winnowing, seems to be indicated in the story that Isis placed the severed remains of Osiris in a corn-sieve.

But whatever may have been the original character of Egyptian worship, there can be no doubt as to the objects which were prominent in it for many generations. Nowhere in the antique world have the death of the body and the life of the soul been matter of so much anxious thought as in Egypt; nowhere have so great efforts been made to preserve for those who have passed away from earth a memory full of honour and regard. The valley of the Nile is a long scroll margined with memorials of the dead. From the river are seen everywhere tombs, sculptured stones, symbols, enigmatic characters. For thousands of years a whole people devoted itself with unremitting assiduity to the task of securing for its kindred a new life beyond the grave. Death should be, they thought, to him who is duly prepared for it but a crisis in life. They regarded, says Diodorus,[30] their houses but as wayside inns, their tombs as their everlasting dwellings; the tomb was not the end of life. And in Egypt, as elsewhere, the power of giving man life after death was ascribed to the same deities which were thought to cause the blade to spring from the seemingly dead seed. Osiris came to be regarded as the monarch of the dead and the guide of souls out of earthly darkness into the blissful realm where they shall have full sight of the divinity without restraint. The departed is in a mystic manner identified with Osiris;[31] in his life he lives. And the departed, united with Osiris, comes to have a place in the bark of the sun; in the great contest of light and darkness he is on the side of light. The journey of the soul through the under-world is identified with that of the sun passing under the earth to reach the eastern horizon. Many are the perils which it has to undergo, and its only safety is in union with Osiris, to ensure which the necessary names and formularies are deposited in the coffin and engraved on the sarcophagus.[32] Many of these survive to bear witness to the faith of the ancient men who wrote them. Thus the worship of the sun is connected with that of the Chthonian powers which cause the revival of vegetative life.

Serapis, Osiris-Apis, seems to be a form of Osiris in the character of the god of the lower world. His worship was developed under the Ptolemies, and was naturally influenced by Hellenic views. It spread rapidly and in the time of Hadrian extended throughout the Roman world, superseding that of Osiris. The corn-measure [33] with which his head is crowned indicates that he too was once a deity of the corn. With his cult is generally associated that of Isis, who came to be regarded as the most universal of goddesses,[34] ruling over things in heaven and things on earth and things under the earth, decreeing life and death, reward and punishment. Egyptian purifications and festivals, Egyptian views of the divine judgment of the dead, deeply touched and impressed surrounding nations. In the early days of the Empire the worship of Isis established itself in all parts of the Roman dominion, and was celebrated in several popular festivals.

Of the manner in which the worship of Isis and Osiris was regarded in the early days of Christianity by a man of inquiring mind and great zeal for religion, we have an interesting specimen in Plutarch's treatise on Isis and Osiris. Plutarch, a Greek and a priest of Apollo at Delphi, expresses generally the contempt natural in such a man for foreign superstitions. Nevertheless he is attracted to the worship of these deities; the defects and deformities of their legends he covers under a decent veil of allegory, and he will by no means admit that they are mere local gods of Egypt; they are the universal divinities, worshipped, under one name or other, by all mankind. It was probably the belief in their universality which drew other thoughtful men to the shrines of Isis and Osiris. The more philosophy advanced, the more men shrank from parcelling out the world to local deities. That which was natural when a foreigner was carefully excluded from the worship of the gods of a nation not his own became unnatural when men were conscious of a common humanity transcending national bounds.

And the worship of Isis and Osiris is illustrated by another document of a very different kind, the Metamorphoses of Apuleius. This is a romance of the most extravagant kind, and it is extremely doubtful how far that which is related of the hero represents a real experience of the author. When it is revealed to Lucius, the hero, time after time, that he must give more money to the priests before he can be initiated, we cannot help suspecting the whole narrative of a certain irony. But we may, notwithstanding, be tolerably certain that what Apuleius says of the mysteries of Isis was generally believed, or at all events was likely to be accepted as truth by his contemporaries; and there is nothing in the story of the initiation —so far as it is revealed—monstrous or even improbable. Apuleius,[35] too, like Plutarch, regards Isis as parent of the universe, mistress of the elements, first offspring of the ages, chief of the heavenly beings, ruling over the sky, the sea, and the things under the earth; the one deity whom the whole world worships under many names, though her true name is Isis the Queen. The worshipper addresses her as "Regina Cœli," and it was no doubt as the compassionate and omnipotent Queen of both worlds that she drew to herself so great a crowd of worshippers.

So far we have been concerned with the Chthonian deities; the same gods cause the fruits of the earth to spring up for the living, and receive the souls of the dead into their invisible realm. In Asia, in Egypt, and in Greece, the powers which give life to the corn and the trees seem to have been identified with those which give to man the soul which makes him what he is. But the most prevalent of all cults was that of the sun. Mithras[36] was the Persian god of light, the light of the body and the light of the mind, typified in the glorious sun who never fails to conquer the powers of darkness. And this great deity not only protected and supported man in this life, but watched over his soul in the next, guarding it from the spirits of evil. His worship, already widely spread in the east, is said to have been introduced into the western provinces in the first century before Christ. In the early part of the second century after Christ it had become common in every part of the Roman Empire; wherever Roman troops were stationed we find traces of Mithraic worship. The great deity was commonly worshipped in a cave, which, originally perhaps representing the recess beneath the earth in which the sun was supposed to hide his beams during the night, came to signify to devout worshippers the abyss into which the soul must descend, to be purified by many trials before leaving it. His worship became a mystery, to which votaries were only admitted after passing through many grades and various trials.

From very early times the deities who presided over vegetation were regarded as having charge also of the souls of men, while the sunlight typified a life more glorious than that of earth. But why did these deities come to be specially looked upon as guardians of souls? No certain and conclusive answer can be given, but we may at any rate say that primitive man drew little or no distinction between the life or spirit of vegetation and the spirit of man.[37] The legends both of the Semitic and the Indo-Germanic race testify to the ancient belief of man that plants and trees were animated by spirits not unlike his own. That men are sprung from plants or trees is an article of belief among some of the African tribes even to this day.

Now, to advance one stage upon this, man might well imagine that, as all plants and trees spring from the earth, some great beings dwelling beneath the earth ruled over the spirits and sent them into the grass and herb and tree which grew up everywhere on its surface.

And if such earth-deities ruled over the spirits of plants and trees, were they not also rulers of the spirits of men, themselves also sprung from trees, or at any rate in some way from the earth? The doctrine of rewards and punishments in the world to come, such as it existed at the time of the first preaching of Christianity, is doubtless a later development, and has received accretions from many quarters; but it may well have been grafted on such a primeval belief as that which I have supposed; and this doctrine was especially prominent in mystic worship.[38]

The various Mysteries differed widely from each other, but certain general characteristics may be traced in all. All required some kind of preparation and purification before admission; in all there were λεγόμενα and δεικνύμενα or δρώμενα, words spoken and actions exhibited; in all it seems certain that an allegoric exposition was given of dramatised story of some deity or deities. And while Olympus was no place for suffering which could mar the bliss of the supernal deities, in the Mysteries the suffering of a god, suffering followed by triumph, seems to have been the invariable subject of the sacred drama. In all, the initiated were led to hope for divine help in this life, atonement for sin past, and an immortality of bliss. And the general tendency of the Mysteries, at least in their later forms, seems to have been towards monotheism; the gods of popular mythology become no more than parts of one stupendous whole, or even mere appellations of the one only God. The Mysteries thus attempted to cover precisely the same ground which was in due time occupied by the Christian Church. They exhibit very strongly those yearnings of humanity which the Incarnation of the Son of God was to satisfy. They were doubtless attractive to the very same class of minds which welcomed Christianity when it was preached to them. Tatian[39] tells us that he had himself been admitted to some Mysteries, but found no satisfaction until he met with certain barbaric books — the Scriptures — at once older and more divine than those of the Greeks. The relation between these Mysteries, whether with regard to teaching or doctrine, and the sacraments of the Christian Church will be the subject of the remaining lectures of this course.

Such claims as those of the Mysteries appealed strongly to a perplexed and troubled age. At the time when Christianity was first preached, the old confident, self-reliant spirit of the Greeks, which was so little afraid of consequences, had almost passed away; philosophers and populace were alike haunted by a consciousness of impurity in the sight of the deity, which led them to seek purification; and by a feeling of spiritual weakness, which rendered the thought of divine help, protection, and guidance inexpressibly grateful to them. The mere performance of rites and recitation of formularies no longer satisfied men who were in this condition of mind; they needed the glow of mystic devotion, the sense of being raised "above the smoke and stir of this dim spot, which men call earth," to a nearer sight of the divinity. In this age we find not only the populace, but philosophers seeking for salvation, σωτηρία; and if this word did not connote all that the word "salvation" does for us, it still acknowledged the need of divine help if men were to become partakers of the divine nature, escaping the taint that is in the world through lust.[40] We find something in Seneca and Plutarch which is not present in the writings of the classic period, not even in those of the most religious of all philosophers, Plato; a consciousness of the perplexities of human life, a readiness to accept help wherever it may be offered, which are by no means characteristic either of Greeks or Romans in the hardy days of vigorous political life. The individual man becomes more important as the greater organism, the city or state, ceases to be all-absorbing.

On minds in this condition the Eastern deities, with their claims to be of primeval antiquity and to impart wisdom unattainable by the natural powers of man, served by priests totally unlike the state-officials who regulated the ceremonies and recited the traditional words at civic festivals, priests who, in many cases at least, held themselves aloof from the ordinary duties of a citizen, and devoted themselves to the service of their sanctuary, priests who often gave themselves out to be the interpreters of a divinity,— on seeking and anxious minds such deities and such priests often made a deep impression. And in particular the secret worship of such deities had a peculiar attraction. Secrecy itself, the privilege of being admitted to a society not open to the common herd, is itself attractive to many minds, and if the mystagogue had in fact little to reveal, it was no doubt commonly believed that he could reveal much. Few men love the narrow road which leads to truth. To pass along the painful path, stumbling and falling, seizing, examining, rejecting things which come before our gaze, retaining at last perhaps but little of all that we once seemed to have, this is delightful to the few choice spirits who are the salt of the earth, but to every-day commonplace minds it is hateful. Many of those who enter on the search for truth, when they encounter its difficulties and discouragements, fall into an easy and seductive scepticism. They ask, "What is truth?" and will not stay for an answer. But there is also a large class always ready to welcome that which offers them truth without the labour and disappointment which the search for it involves. It was this feeling which drew crowds to those secret associations which offered, by certain words and ceremonies, to put them in possession of the absolute truth as to man and his destinies. To have the great secret which men so much desire, and in the search for which they go so widely astray, whispered in their ears by one who had learned it from the divinity; to be set on a pinnacle of knowledge above the crowd of the blind and ignorant;—this could not but be enchanting. No wonder that in the early days of the Empire, when the minds of men were so deeply moved by the thought of man's lot when he passed to that bourne whence no traveller returns, when hierophants of ancient rites, and shameless impostors who imitated their craft, were everywhere found, crowds were drawn to the various initiations—crowds of men who were often, no doubt, disillusioned and disappointed.

Such men are always destined to be disillusioned. Truth cannot be poured into the mind as we pour wine into a goblet; the attainment of it is as much due to the training of the mind as to that which is imparted from without. When a man is admitted into the Church of Christ, it is not pretended that he is at once put in possession of all truth, but he has imparted to him *fruitful* truths — truths which will enable him to bring forth fruit unto holiness and to attain finally everlasting life. He is made partaker of that special gift of the Spirit which will in the end, if he is faithful to it, guide him into all truth; but even an Apostle, while he is yet surrounded by the trials and perplexities of this life, "counts not himself to have apprehended" the whole truth; there is still something to know; he stretches forward still, "that he may know Christ and the power of His resurrection, and the fellow-ship of His sufferings, being conformed unto His death; if by any means He might attain unto the resurrection from the dead." Such is the course of every one who is initiated into the secret of Christ. "The Word was made flesh and dwelt among us"; "in Him was life, and the life was the light of men." Simple words, but words of divine origin and of divine force. May God grant us grace so to live by them that we may in the end rise above the darkness of our present state, and dwell in His everlasting light.

LECTURE III

III

"Howbeit we speak wisdom among the perfect: yet a wisdom not of this world, nor of the rulers of this world, which are coming to nought: but we speak God's wisdom in a mystery, even the wisdom that hath been hidden, which God foreordained before the worlds unto our glory."—
1 COR. ii. 6, 7. (R.V.)

THE general result of our brief survey of the chief pagan Mysteries is this. At the time when the Christian Church was making its early conquests, the Empire was covered with Mysteries, or with what much resembled Mysteries, Thiasi, associations formed for the worship of some deity distinct from the civic gods of the countries where they were formed. It is hardly too much to say with Renan that these formed the serious part of pagan religion. The yearning of paganism sought in them what it had not found in the national cult, and the lovers of the old paganism hoped to find in them a defence against victorious Christianity. As Christianity advanced, there seems to have been an attempt to render the Mysteries more attractive and more impressive to the new forms of thought which had arisen. The Mysteries doubtless shared in the pagan revival under Hadrian and the Antonines. The former was indeed himself initiated into the Eleusinian.

Now, what influence did the ancient societies which, under whatever name, attempted to satisfy the deep craving in the mind of man for purification and the hope of a blessed immortality, exert upon the rising Church in its early years? Preller,[41] to whose investigations I owe much, says that in the struggle with paganism, Christianity "did not win its victory without receiving some wounds of which it even now bears the scars; for careful and extensive research would certainly show that much of that which in the Catholic Church (whether Roman or Greek) is not derived from the Gospel, particularly as regards ritual, is to be referred to that contest, and to be regarded as spoil from the pagan Mysteries taken over into the enemy's camp." Renan [42] adopts this sentence, and adds,

"The primitive form of Christian worship was a mystery. All the internal discipline of the Church, the grades of initiation, the injunction of secrecy, numerous peculiar ecclesiastical terms, have no other origin." And an English writer of remarkable ability and great learning, whose premature death no one lamented more than I, the late Dr. Hatch, expressed the same sentiment with somewhat greater definiteness.[43] " The influence of the Mysteries," he says, "and of the religious cults which were analogous to the Mysteries, was not simply general; they modified in some important respects the Christian sacraments of Baptism and the Eucharist —the practice, that is, of admission to the society by a symbolical purification, and the practice of expressing membership of the society by a common meal. . . . The elements which are found in the later and not in the earlier form [of the sacraments] are elements which are found outside Christianity in the [Mysteries and Thiasi]."

It seems worth while to examine how far this allegation is true. That it contains some truth few candid inquirers would, I think, be disposed to deny. A society for worship, a society seeking to enlist among its members not only scions of one race or citizens of one city, but all men everywhere, without distinction of race or sex or condition, could scarcely fail to resemble in general traits societies already founded with a similar aim and under similar circumstances. The question is, How far did the resemblance extend? How much of it was due to direct imitation? How much was due to influences within the body itself?

In this inquiry we must bear in mind that we are not concerned with words, but things. When Mysteries were everywhere found, their terminology naturally came to be commonly employed, and to be applied to matters altogether foreign to its original usage. Plato[44] frequently uses words referring to initiation in the Mysteries to designate the introduction of the neophyte into the light of divine philosophy, and such words came also to be applied to medicine and other branches of physical science and to political knowledge. Nay, in the time of Cicero, one who conducted strangers over the public buildings of a city was called a mystagogue.⁴⁵ When the word was so used, it can scarcely have recalled the idea of a Mystery more than the word "Kapellmeister," applied to the conductor of a band, recalls the notion of a chapel. The use of such words as μύστης and μεμυημένος in later times may be compared to our use of the word "adept." Not more than two hundred years ago it distinctly suggested the alchemists or Rosicrucians; now, who that speaks of an adept in some art or some game dreams of its connection with old pseudo-science? We must therefore be cautious in inferring from the mere use of a word that a corresponding institution accompanied it.

And terms which designate Christian rites have sometimes been over-hastily referred for their origin to pagan Mysteries. "So early as the time of Justin Martyr, we find," it is said,⁴⁶ "a name given to baptism which comes straight from the Greek Mysteries — the name 'enlightenment' (φωτισμός, φωτίζεσθαι)." It is quite true that Justin applies the word "enlightenment" to the sacred font, because he says "it implies that the minds of the baptized have been enlightened by previous instruction"; but it is very doubtful whether initiation into a Mystery is described by pagans as φωτισμός.[47] The Christian use of the word φωτισμός is derived in the most obvious and natural way from the contrast between the state of those who had become "light in the Lord," "children of light," and that of the men who were still in darkness. The word σφραγίς, seal, applied to baptism and especially to the sign of the cross, is said to come "both from the Mysteries and from some forms of foreign cult"; but in the instances given in support of this the seal is simply the seal of the lips, the seal of silence, while it is evident that when the "seal" is applied to Christian baptism it is the seal of the covenant, or perhaps, as Gregory of Nazianzus[48] suggests, the token of the service of the divine Master.

We must remember, too, how fragmentary and imperfect is our knowledge both of the Mysteries and of the forms of Christian worship in the second century after Christ, the age in which so much was formed which comes into light for us only in the later age of which the literary remains are abundant. If two ancient frescoes are discovered, much defaced, a few dexterous touches may make them resemble each other, though when both were perfect they may have been totally unlike. I am disposed to think that some rhetorical dexterity has been employed in tracing the resemblances between the pagan and the Christian mysteries.

Again, the relations of the pagan and Christian Mysteries are sometimes treated as if it was impossible for the later developments of paganism to have been due to a desire to adopt what was seen to be attractive in Christianity. And yet we can hardly doubt that the same feeling, which in after years led Julian to attempt to remodel pagan institutions after the pattern of Christian, must have tempted earlier pagans, when they saw with dismay the constant growth of Christianity, to offer, so far as they could, the same attractions which drew men to the worship of the Church.[49]

That which has especially struck most modern inquirers into the nature of the Mysteries is their secrecy, or supposed secrecy, as to their rites, a point which to an ancient philosopher probably seemed the most natural thing in the world. It was at any rate the fact that the rites or exhibitions within the sacred precinct were only displayed to the initiated, and it is often represented that the practice of keeping secret certain portions of Christian worship and doctrine from the world at large, and only revealing them with precaution to certain disciples who, after long trial, were judged worthy, is alien from the original spirit of Christianity, and is due probably to the influence of the pagan Mysteries. "It is possible," we read,[50] "that they made the Christian associations more secret than before. Up to a certain time there is no evidence that Christianity had any secrets. It was preached openly to the world. It guarded worship by imposing a moral bar to admission. But its rites were simple, and its teaching was public. After a certain time all is changed; mysteries have arisen in the once open and easily accessible faith, and there are doctrines which must not be declared in the hearing of the uninitiated."

Now, we may say at once that the early Christians took nothing consciously from pagan Mysteries. They felt for them a repugnance and abhorrence even greater than for other pagan institutions.[51] Whether their horror was justified is not now the question; we are only concerned with the fact, of which there is abundant evidence.

But, further, there seems to be a certain confusion in the statement which I have just quoted. To allow none but those who had learned the truths of Christianity, and had been duly admitted to the Church by baptism, to be present at the most solemn rite of Christians, is one thing; to practise reserve in teaching is another. To speak first of the former. I can see no reason to believe that the Holy Eucharist, having at first been free and open to all, became, under the influence of the pagan Mysteries, close and secret. Though the Gospel is proclaimed to all men, it by no means follows that every act of worship within the Church should be open to the infidel as well as to the true believer. The king sends forth his servants to bid all men to the marriage-feast, and yet he will not have them sit down in garments soiled and stained in the ways of the world. That which is holy is not to be given to dogs, nor pearls to those who in their swinish mood would trample them under their feet. Christianity has, in fact, always been anxious to guard its treasures from profanation.

There is no reason to believe that at any time during the first four centuries unbaptized persons were present during the most solemn part of the eucharistic office. All the precedents of the ancient world, not of the Mysteries only, were against the indiscriminate admission of worshippers. Among the Jews, the entrance of Gentiles into the court in which sacrifice was offered was forbidden on pain of death; at the Jewish Passover only the members of a Jewish family, natural or adoptive, could be present. But to the synagogues, the main purpose of which was rather instruction than worship,[52] the uncircumcised were freely admitted, and often formed a large part of the congregation. It is precisely analogous to this that unbaptized persons were permitted to be present at that portion of the Christian offices which consisted, like the synagogue services, of lections, exposition, and prayer for common mercies, though not at the celebration of the Eucharist.

In the Gentile world only citizens could be present at a civic sacrifice, and those who formed associations for the worship of a foreign deity took care that it should be accessible only to the associates.

When Christianity came into the world, doubtless the salvation offered by God in Christ was preached with the most complete openness and freedom; all men were entreated to enter the fold; but it by no means follows that all men were at once admitted to the rite which the Lord instituted in the midst of the small body of those who had companied with Him all the time of His ministry, and learned the lessons of His divine school. When the Breaking of Bread took place in private houses we may be sure that none but the faithful witnessed it. At Corinth an ἰδιώτης, not gifted with tongues, or even an ἄπιστος, one in no sense belonging to the fold of Christ, might be present in a meeting at which the gifts of prophesying or of tongues were exercised; but there is nothing to connect this meeting with the Eucharist, which is mentioned separately in the same epistle in a different connection; and here the Apostle certainly seems to speak only of Christians, the flock whom he addresses, as coming together. Pliny,[53] when he inquired about the Bithynian Church, knew nothing of what took place in Christian assemblies except what he learned from Christians. Not even spies seem to have succeeded in mingling with the worshippers. In fact, the very calumnies which were current as to what took place when Christians met show how carefully their secret was kept. It is the unknown region that is peopled with monsters.

The question, Who were allowed to be *present* at the celebration of the Holy Eucharist? is distinct from the question, What *knowledge* had those who were without of the rites of those who were within the pale? As to the latter, St. Paul's Epistles and the Gospels, or—at a still earlier date—the materials from which the Gospels were drawn, must have been accessible to all who wished to read them. We must not indeed suppose that the sending forth of such books as these resembled the printing and publishing of a modern book. Books such as St. Paul's letters, intended for the use of particular churches or of individuals, would probably at first be little, if at all, known beyond the circle to which they were addressed. And the Gospels would probably find few readers outside the Christian Church. They were written by Christians for Christians. Still, an eager pagan inquirer like Celsus, in the second century, had no difficulty in making himself acquainted with the leading facts of the Gospel history; and what Celsus could do, other pagans might also do. In the fourth century, when the secrecy of some portions of the sacred rites is constantly spoken of, books were multiplied, and such authorities as St. John Chrysostom[54] speak as if domestic reading of the New Testament was common. Books which were commonly found in private houses can scarcely have been entirely out of the reach of any who wished to read them. We may assume, therefore, that the general nature of Christian rites may have been known to many who were not Christians. And yet there may have been something in the manner of celebrating the Eucharist which Christians wished to conceal, and did conceal, from those who were not initiated and sealed. Some gesture which it was believed the Lord had used, the actual form of εὐλογία, the actual form of εὐχαριστία—these remain unrevealed in the writings of the New Testament. These, we may well believe, were concealed from the knowledge of those who were without, lest profane use should be made of them. And we may say much the same of the Apologists. They indeed, in books addressed to pagans, tell us much of the celebration of the most sacred rite of Christianity; but their descriptions also, like those of the Gospels and of St. Paul, are quite general. There is no mention of the gestures used, no quoting the words of εὐλογία or εὐχαριστία. St. Basil,[55] in the fourth century, asks which of the saints left behind for us in writing the words of the epiclesis, the invocation of the Holy Spirit upon the elements, which was regarded as highly important for the mystery. Such an epiclesis is in fact found in all Liturgies except the Roman, and in the East is regarded as essential to consecration. But no Apologist gives it; and I think that it would be difficult to show from the Apologists that the words of institution, to which so great importance is attached in the West, were recited over the elements. And yet the use of these words is so absolutely universal in Liturgies that it is almost impossible to doubt that it is primitive. The profanation which Christians most dreaded was a mock celebration by unbelievers; hence they carefully avoided revealing the sacred words to which special efficacy was attributed. The secrecy of Christian worship arose from the circumstances under which it came into the world.

The rites of the Church were no doubt much more simple in the days when worship was held in the upper room of a faithful disciple than it is now, when it is practically open to all. Publicity and splendour have almost certainly advanced with equal steps. But on this we need not dwell, for all are agreed as to the fact of the increase in the splendour and complexity of ritual, to whatever cause they may attribute it. The question which I wish to discuss is, How far is it true that "mysteries have arisen"—let us say in the fourth century—"in the once open and easily accessible faith, and there are doctrines which must not be declared in the hearing of the uninitiated."

We admit at once the perfect simplicity, frankness, and fulness of the first preachers of the Gospel. They were ἄνθρωποι ἀγράμματοι καὶ ἰδιῶται, men neither specially trained in literature nor teachers by profession. When they speak of the mystery of God, the mysteries of the kingdom of heaven, and the like, they do not speak of something to be carefully kept secret, to be revealed as a great privilege to a chosen few. Far from it. They speak of something to be proclaimed with the loud voice of a herald throughout the world, of glad tidings to be brought to every creature; they go forth into the world to bring to the wretched and degraded tidings of great joy, of a new birth unto righteousness. Their message was not to a select aristocracy of the wise and learned, like that of a Greek philosopher or a Hebrew rabbi; they had no contempt for the untaught multitude; on the contrary, it was to the despised and despairing class that their words especially came home. True, that which they had to proclaim was a mystery, a secret for long ages hidden; but once made known, it was to be hidden no more. The secret of godliness is of One who was manifested in the flesh, justified in the spirit, seen of angels, proclaimed or heralded among the nations, believed on in the world, received up in glory. This is a truth which man could not reach by any exertion of the intellect; here the imaginative spirit of Plato is as powerless as the dull mind of the slave at the mill. That which the first preachers of the Gospel proclaimed was a secret revealed, and I do not know that it was ever attempted to obscure it. Granting, as of course we do grant, that in the third century something was revealed only to those who had been carefully trained to receive it, what, after all, was it which was not proclaimed in the streets and lanes? To the charge that Christians veiled in silence many of their principles Origen[59] replied with much force, that in fact the doctrines of Christians were much better known in the world than the tenets of philosophers. Who, he says, has not heard of Jesus the virgin-born, the crucified? Who knows not His resurrection, and the judgment to come, in which sinners are to be punished and the righteous rewarded according to their deserts? These things were preached to all who would hear; and how does this preaching differ from that of St. Paul, when he preached Jesus and the resurrection, when he reasoned of righteousness and self-control and the judgment to come? Certainly he taught even higher things than these, but it was to those who were full-grown, not to babes in Christ, not to curious triflers like the Athenians, nor to "rulers of this world" like Felix, that he proclaimed "the wisdom of God in a mystery, the wisdom which had been hidden." Thus, in the Christian as in the pagan mysteries, while the general objects of the teaching—the revelation of God in Christ, His resurrection, and the blessedness of those who faithfully follow Him—were known to all without any concealment or diminution, some forms of ritual, and some points of doctrine which were not at once intelligible, were reserved for those who had been specially prepared to receive them. That persons brought up in a Christian family were ignorant of Christian truth until they had passed through the catechumenate is a hypothesis which cannot be maintained for an instant.

Reticence on certain high matters of Christian doctrine was probably occasioned, at least in part, by consideration for the pagans themselves. In the end, doubtless, Christian doctrine found expression in a manner not only intelligible but attractive to the Greek spirit, but at first, as we may see in such thinkers as Marcus Aurelius and Celsus, there was something in its teaching which an unimpassioned and unsympathetic pagan found difficult to grasp; something which was to him foolishness, as being out of harmony with his way of regarding man and nature. Now, teaching which is above the range of the ordinary thought of cultivated men, and yet is too important to be neglected, is sure to be the butt of the artillery of nimble wits in every age. It was therefore natural enough that Christians should shrink from exposing their most abstruse doctrines to the mockery of pagans who might in the end bitterly repent it. Mockery of this kind would be to them blasphemy—blasphemy which would hurt both him that spoke and him that heard.[57]

Whatever the motive, it is clear that certain formularies of worship and certain expressions of doctrine were only revealed to those who were on the point of receiving Holy Baptism. This fact gave great importance to the preliminary training of the catechumens.

That as early as the end of the second century candidates for baptism passed through a course of instruction before they were admitted to the full privileges of their calling is certainly established, though the fuller development of the sytem belongs to the fourth. At this time the formularies of the baptismal rite itself, the Creed or confession of faith, the Lord's Prayer, the form of consecrating and administering the Holy Eucharist, were only made known to the postulants at the end of their course of instruction. They were divided into two [58]—or possibly more—classes. A course of instruction preparatory to baptism is sometimes thought to be of post-apostolic origin, and the division into classes to resemble the degrees of initiation in some of the pagan Mysteries. And yet that persons under instruction should be divided into classes, and advanced from one to the other according to their proficiency, is a matter so very simple and obvious as hardly to require a precedent. As Lobeck says, every one has to approach the end at which he aims by steps;[59] there is no other way.

"In the earliest times (we read)[60] baptism followed at once upon conversion. . . . This is shown by the Acts of the Apostles; the men who repented at Pentecost, those who believed when Philip preached in Samaria, the Ethiopian eunuch, Cornelius, Lydia, the jailer at Philippi, the converts at Corinth and Ephesus, were baptized as soon as they were known to recognise Jesus as the Messiah." Jews and Jewish proselytes were no doubt baptized as soon as they declared their faith in Jesus as the Messiah. They already knew the Scriptures; they acknowledged the Father and the Holy Spirit; what they needed for the completeness of their faith was but the recognition of the Son who redeemeth us. The multitudes who believed after the first Pentecost, Cornelius, Lydia, and the Ethiopian eunuch were so admitted. Probably the same might be said of the Samaritans, but in fact we do not know what instruction they received before they were baptized. The narrative gives the impression that Philip's preaching continued for some time before the baptisms began. We know nothing of the instruction given to Gentile converts at Corinth, but we cannot doubt that before baptism they were at any rate sufficiently instructed to be enabled to understand what was meant when it was said that Jesus of Nazareth was the anointed One, the promised Messiah; and this, for persons who started from purely pagan training, implies a course of teaching neither brief nor perfunctory. Those who were baptized at Ephesus had been instructed by the Alexandrian Jew Apollos, a man not only mighty in Scripture, but bubbling over with the Spirit, and himself taught in the way of the Lord. Is it conceivable that such a man had failed to teach them to believe in the Father and the Holy Spirit, according to the conception current among the more enlightened Jews, though he had not told them of the special gift of the Holy Ghost, which was the consequence of the ascension of the Son to the Father? Of the Philippian jailer nothing is known; he may have been a Jew or a proselyte. But whatever may have been the primitive practice, it is certain that before the end of the second century a regular system of instruction was provided for those who desired to be baptized. In primitive times this instruction seems to have been mainly of a practical kind, intended to impress upon the candidate the great and awful distinction between the way of life and the way of death; but as it is not disputed that from the first men were baptized into the name of the Father and of the Son and of the Holy Ghost, it is inconceivable that any should have been brought to the sacred font who had not been taught the doctrine of the Holy Three in One, the essence of the Christian creed; and this implies, at any rate for Gentiles, a course of instruction, probably of considerable length. Whatever else it may have contained, it must have supplied an answer to the question, "What think ye of

Christ?" To that extent it must have been dogmatic from the first. As theology became more careful and elaborate, doubtless instruction became less simple; it became in the middle of the fourth century such as we see it in the Catechetical Lectures of Cyril of Jerusalem; but the great central dogma must always have been taught. And to this dogmatic teaching the Mysteries can offer no parallel. Paganism had no dogmas—propositions, that is, on theological subjects enforced by authority, to the exclusion of all others. Theology, indeed, it had in abundance, but it was not the affair of priests and hierophants, but of philosophers, and of these no one sect could claim the sole possession of orthodoxy. Stoics and Epicureans alike might, if they chose, approach the shrines of their country's deities. Nothing which we should call faith was required of them, but only observance. Any resemblance, therefore, between the preparation for admission to the Christian Church and the preparation for admission to the pagan Mysteries must be purely superficial, and it may well be doubted whether there is even a superficial resemblance.

It can scarcely be seriously maintained that the numerous trials through which (it is said) the candidate for Mithraic initiation had to pass, have any analogy within the Church ; and the eight degrees of the Mithraic initiated, with their fantastic designations of ravens, fighters, lions, and the like, are in flagrant contrast with the absolute equality of those who have learned the secret of Christ.[60] In any case, the development of Mithraism, in the form with which we are concerned, is so exactly contemporary with the development of the Christian Church, that if there were any resemblance, it would be difficult to say which was the imitation and which the original.

LECTURE IV

II

IV

> "I am come a light into the world, that whosoever believeth on me may not abide in the darkness."—ST. JOHN xii. 46. (R.V.)

THEON of Smyrna,[61] in the second century after Christ, tells us that there were five grades or degrees of initiation into the Mysteries. "First, the preliminary purification (καθαρμός), for not all who wish are allowed to partake of the Mysteries, but proclamation is made to exclude from them some men as not having pure hands or discreet lips, and those who are not excluded must receive purification before proceeding further. Secondly, after the purification (κάθαρσιν) comes the transmission of the mystic secret or symbol (ἡ τῆς τελετῆς παράδοσις). Thirdly, what is called full vision (ἐποπτεία). Fourthly, what is indeed the completion of the ἐποπτεία, the weaving of garlands and placing them on the head, so that a man would be able to hand on to others the mystic secret which he has received if he is appointed a torch-bearer or a hierophant, or to any other sacred office. Fifthly, the blessedness ($εὐδαιμονία$) arising from what has gone before, in accordance with the gods' will, and in harmony with their life."

It is evident that in this passage Theon, in fact, describes no more than three stages, for the crowning is but an adjunct of ἐποπτεία, and the blessedness is a condition of mind induced by the initiation and the subsequent vision.

Clement of Alexandria[62] speaks in a similar strain, telling us that the purifying rites come first in the Hellenic Mysteries, as the bath does among the barbarians. Next after these come the lesser Mysteries, laying a foundation of teaching and of preparation for what is to come.

We may note here that the purifying rite of which Clement speaks was not simply the washing of water, for he distinguishes the purifying of the Hellenic Mysteries from the bath of the barbarians; the καθάρσια, whatever they were, preceded the ceremonies, as the λοῦτρον did among the barbarians. They could not themselves be that to which they are compared.

Further, no instruction is mentioned as preceding the purifying rites. All that (according to Theon) precedes the pagan purification is the proclamation to the unclean to avoid presenting themselves. There were, or there might be, degrees of initiation *after* this.

In the Christian Church there was a long preparation for the purifying rite of Baptism; with the pagans some kind of ceremonial purification was the first step towards initiation, and for this no preparation was required but an easy abstinence for a few days.[63]

But further, pagan purification rested upon a wholly different conception of human life from that of the Christian. "It was not," says Rohde,[64] "a heartfelt consciousness of sin, not a moral sense in pain that the purifying rite had to assuage; rather, it was the superstitious dread of a world of spirits, hovering over men with eerie presence, and clutching at them with a thousand hands out of the dim obscurity, which called for the help of the purifier and the atoning priest." It was not merely as a preliminary to the Mysteries that purification was required; some kind of cleansing was commonly required before the worshipper could take part in any sacred rite. And this was not all; uncleanness might be contracted by circumstances of the most trivial kind; from eating a particular kind of food, for instance, or even from seeing another eat it.[65] Nothing is more curious than the lists in Theophrastus and Plutarch[66] of the trifling mishaps from the effects of which a superstitious man required to be cleansed, often by what Plutarch calls impure purifications and unclean cleansings. For it was not merely the washing of water that was used for ceremonial purifying; strange rites, such as rubbing with clay or bran, were resorted to under the pressure of superstitious fear even in the midst of Greek and Roman civilisation. In many cases the conception of the defilement incurred seems little else than material. Many of the philosophers had, no doubt, far more adequate conceptions of the flesh, with its affections and lusts, but they sought purification not in things external, not in lustral waters or magic words, but in the plain living and high thinking which might raise them above the meanness and vileness of the sordid crowd.

The purifications of the pagan world were occasional, employed to remove uncleanness contracted in the ordinary course of life, or to fit men for taking part in some solemn ceremonial, such as sacrifice or the celebration of Mysteries. They resembled the ceremonial cleansings of the Levitical law much more than anything found in the Christian Church. But we find that in the second century after Christ the completion of initiation into the Mysteries of Isis was regarded as conferring a new life on the votary, and placing him in the way of salvation; he was born again (renatus) and blessed (beatus).[67] Whether this usage was derived from terms already in use in the Christian Church it is impossible to say.

Tertullian,[68] however, found a very exact counterpart of Christian baptism in pagan rites. The devil, he says, "baptizes some, of course such as believe in him and are faithful to him; he promises expiation of sins from the bath, and, if my memory of Mithras serves me still, in this rite he signs his soldiers on their foreheads." The rest of the passage does not at present concern us. In the expressions about the ceremonial bath Tertullian adds nothing to our knowledge. We know, probably better than he did, how universal in paganism was the washing of water as a sign of purification from some taint of crime or sin. But when he speaks of signing on the forehead he describes a ceremony absolutely identical with one used, if not primitively, certainly in very ancient times, in Christian baptism, so far, that is, as regards the use of some sign, for it is not clear what the Mithraic sign was. It should, however, be observed that Tertullian is the only authority for this "signing," and that he speaks as if he had no great confidence in the accuracy of his memory. It is perhaps too much to say with Fabri[69] that the story is undoubtedly a fiction, but we certainly ought not to build a theory on an isolated and doubtful testimony. Moreover, we ought not to lose sight of the possibility that at the end of the second century paganism may have imitated Christianity.

Clement of Alexandria, in the passage

already quoted, tells us that the purifying ceremony was followed by the lesser Mysteries, which, he says, "contain some groundwork of teaching and of preparation for what is to follow." This seems to be identical with Theon's "delivery of initiation." What this teaching and preparation was no man knows. Lobeck,[70] than whom there is no higher authority, says of it, that whether it consisted merely of the sight of sacred objects, or of precepts and admonitions, and (if the latter), to what they related, whether to the conduct of life or the observance of ceremonies, "latet æternumque latebit," hid is it now and hid will ever be. But as the same word παράδοσις is used of the delivery of the Creed to the catechumens before their baptism, the two rites are sometimes compared. The similarity consists simply in this, that in each case something is brought to the knowledge of the candidate of which he was before ignorant, and that as a qualification for something further. When certain points of Christian doctrine and worship were revealed only to those who were judged fit to receive them, some such imparting of the knowledge hitherto concealed there needs must be, and it could hardly fail to have at any rate a superficial resemblance to the similar ceremony in the Mysteries.

The Creed, once imparted, became the watchword of the Christian soldier, by which he distinguished his comrades in the great warfare. "Every leader," says Rufinus,[1] "gives to his soldiers distinctive watchwords, in order that if one is met with of whose character there is doubt, he may, on being asked the watchword, show whether he is friend or foe." The Christian soldier makes his solemn promise of allegiance to the great Captain, and the word "sacramentum" testifies how the military metaphor impressed itself on the language of the Church. Even to this day we pray that the neophyte may not be ashamed to confess the faith of Christ crucified, and manfully to fight under His banner against sin, the world, and the devil, and to continue Christ's faithful soldier and servant unto his life's end. There can be little doubt that it was from the military vocabulary that the word σύμβολον was taken when it was applied to the Creed. So it is said,[72] "those who were admitted to the inner sights of the Mysteries had a formula or password (σύμβολον or σύνθημα)." This was no doubt the case; members of associations for worship had means of recognising each other; sometimes passwords, sometimes actual objects which might be exhibited.[73]

"Just as the divinities watched the initiated from out of the blaze of light, so Chrysostom pictures Christian baptism in the blaze of Easter Eve; and Cyril describes the white-robed band of the baptized approaching the doors of the church where the lights turned darkness into day."[74] In the pagan Mysteries the postulant seems to have passed through darkness and terrors on his way to the sacred scenes which were displayed. The purpose of this was probably to enhance the effect of the mystic dramatic scenes, but a symbolic meaning was no doubt attributed to it. Apuleius[75] says that in his initiation into the Isiac Mysteries he drew near the bounds of death, and after treading the threshold of Proserpine saw at midnight the sun shining with a brilliant light;

he approached and worshipped the gods above and the gods below, their statues or their representatives standing forth, doubtless, in the blaze as of noonday. The use of light in the ceremonies of Christian baptism was of a different kind. In the first place, it was not the case that—as seems to be implied in the passage quoted above—the baptized approached through darkness "the doors of the church where the light turned darkness into day." They were themselves the bringers of light; each neophyte carried a lamp or taper. And this constitutes a marked distinction from the pagan ceremony; for in the Mysteries the torch-bearer (δᾳδοῦχος) was an official of considerable importance, which he scarcely could have been if all the initiated bore lights. Moreover, we do not hear of baptismal lights before the fourth century, when the Mysteries could have had but little influence. Lights were rendered necessary by the custom of holding the great baptismal festival of the year in the night preceding Easter-Day; once adopted, they soon received a symbolical meaning, and came to typify the kingdom of light to which the neophytes had just been solemnly admitted. There is a very striking description in St. Cyril's Lectures of the scene at Jerusalem on Easter-Eve, when the white-robed band of the newly-baptized streamed from the baptistery to the church of the Resurrection, and the darkness was turned into day by the brightness of unnumbered lights. Angels' voices might well be thought to join in the chant, Blessed are they whose unrighteousness is forgiven and whose sin is covered.[76] It is scarcely credible that the scene in the church, where nothing like a dramatic representation, but only the circle of clergy round the holy table, prepared to celebrate the mystery of divine love, and the solemn yet simple preparations for the commemoration of the Lord's death and resurrection, met the eye on entrance, can have resembled in any degree the scene which greeted the initiated in the Mysteries of Isis or Demeter. In the church all is pure and noble. Surely a ceremonial which made men realise that they were joined to the blessed company of saints and angels was different in kind from a representation of the often impure acts of gods and goddesses, however artfully they may have been allegorised.

"The baptized were sometimes crowned with a garland, as the initiated wore a mystic crown at Eleusis."[77] The earliest reference to this practice, however, is of the seventh century, when the celebration of pagan Mysteries had ceased, and so could not offer a model for Christian. In any case, we need not seek in the Mysteries a precedent for so natural and so widespread a festal adornment as a garland placed on the head. Probably its association with pagan festivities prevented its adoption by Christians until after the abolition of paganism.

On the Eucharist, even in its earliest form, the pagan Mysteries have been supposed to have exercised a great influence. Professor Percy Gardner, to whom we are indebted for much light thrown on Hellenic archæology, holds that the Eucharist originated with St. Paul, and asks us to "suppose that it was in a vision that the comparison of the bread and wine of a banquet to the body and blood of the Lord came before St. Paul."[78] It appears, however, that we are asked to believe that much more than a "comparison" came before St. Paul; we are asked to believe that a vision of a scene on the last evening of the Lord's life came before him, and that so vividly that he accepted it for genuine history, though (by the hypothesis) he had never heard a word of any such scene from the disciples whom he had met with after his conversion. Further, we are asked to believe that Paul, the object of so much suspicion to a large portion of the brethren, succeeded in imposing his vision as sober fact upon the whole Church, Jewish and Gentile alike, at a time when many men were still living who had been with the Lord during His whole ministry, until the time when He was taken up into heaven. This can scarcely be said to be a plausible hypothesis. Further, we are told[70] that "the pagan ceremonies which offered the closest parallel to the sacred feast of the *Corinthian Epistle* were certainly the Mysteries," and that "the central point of the ceremonial at Eleusis appears to have been a sacred repast of which the initiated partook, and by means of which they had communion with the gods." If St. Paul had a vision of a sacred feast instituted by Christ, it is surely infinitely more probable that his imagination would be influenced by his remembrance of the breaking of bread and the blessing of cups in the Passover, with which he had been familiar from childhood, than by the Mysteries of Eleusis, of which he could have known nothing but the current gossip; for it is not suggested, and it would in any case be incredible, that he was initiated. But further, if there is anything certain about the Eleusinian Mysteries, it is that "the central point of the ceremonial" was a drama. The only passage referred to in confirmation of the statement in the text is Clemens Alex. *Cohort. ad Gentes*, p. 18 (Potter). But neither there nor elsewhere do we find anything described in the smallest degree resembling the Breaking of the Bread and the Blessing of the Cup. In the passage cited Clement is speaking of the catchword of the Eleusinian Mystæ, which relates apparently solely to the initiatory ceremonies: " I fasted, I drank the cyceon, I took out of the chest, after tasting I put away in the basket (or vase), and from the basket into the chest."[80] The same phrase is given in Latin by Arnobius (*Adv. Nation.* v. 26, p. 198, ed. Reifferscheid), where the words are said to be "symbola quæ rogati sacrorum in acceptionibus respondetis." This might very well mean that the recital of these words was held to prove that the person who uttered them had passed the preliminary stage of initiation. Lobeck takes them to be a response which the candidates were taught to utter. In any case they describe something distinct from, and preliminary to, the "sacrorum acceptio," which is no doubt correlative to ἡ τῆς τελετῆς παράδοσις in Theon, and "traditio sacrorum" in Apuleius. At the time when the postulant drank the cyceon, and so forth, he was not fully initiated. He was taught to refer to the preliminary ceremony at the time of the delivery of the sacra, which again led on to the highest stage, ἐποπτεία, or full vision. The drinking of the cyceon, with its accompanying rites, was thus as different as possible from the Christian Communion, which is the highest privilege of the τέλειοι, or fully initiated.

Dr. Hatch also refers to the drinking of the

cyceon as a kind of communion. "Sometimes," he says,[81] "the baptized received the communion at once after baptism, just as those who had been initiated at Eleusis proceeded at once, after a day's fast, to drink of the mystic κυκεών, and to eat of the sacred cakes." There is no doubt that in the period with which we are concerned the neophyte received the Holy Communion immediately after baptism, and that fasting. There is also no doubt that the votaries at Eleusis, as we have seen, partook of the drink called κυκεών, and of certain mystic cakes taken from a chest or casket, but that this ceremony was in any way a communion is by no means evident. It seems to have taken place once for all, as appears above, at initiation; the phrase is not πίνω, but ἔπιον τὸν κυκεῶνα, a form of speech which could scarcely be used except of an isolated act. In the myth of the origin of the custom of drinking the cyceon it marks the end of Demeter's sorrow and the beginning of a brighter life. It was probably, therefore, intended to symbolise the fuller and more cheering life for which the initiated might hope. It is, in fact, much more analogous to the milk and honey which were put to the lips of the newly baptized than to the "chalice of the grapes of God." In truth, it is a kind of perversity to seek a precedent for Holy Communion in the mystic draught of cyceon when the earth is full of true and real precedents. For the essence of the Sacrament is not merely partaking of a common cup or a common meal, but feasting upon a sacrifice in the benefit of which all the worshippers have a share, and this was found everywhere, among Jews and Gentiles alike. It needs no words of mine to show that the Hebrews feasted upon their sacrifices. In the fifteenth century a learned Jew, Abarbanel,[82] noticed that the Gentiles also followed the same custom. In ancient times, he says, whoever sacrificed to idols made a feast upon the sacrifice. This assertion is perfectly in accordance with the results of modern research. But here let me use the admirable words of Dr. Jevons[83]: "Sacrifice and the sacramental meal which followed on it are institutions which are, or have been, universal. The sacramental meal wherever it exists testifies to man's desire for the closest union with his God, and to his consciousness of the fact that it is upon such union alone that right social relations with his fellow-men can be set. But before there can be a sacramental meal there must be a sacrifice. That is to say, the whole human race for thousands of years has been educated to the conception that it was only through a divine sacrifice that perfect union with God was possible for man. At times the sacramental conception of sacrifice appeared to be about to degenerate entirely into the gift theory; but then, in the sixth century B.C., the sacramental conception woke into new life, this time in the form of a search for a perfect sacrifice — a search which led Clement and Cyprian to try all the mysteries of Greece in vain. But of all the great religions of the world it is the Christian Church alone which is so far heir of all the ages as to fulfil the dumb, dim expectation of mankind; in it alone the sacramental meal commemorates, by ordinance of its Founder, the divine sacrifice which is a propitiation for the sins of all mankind."

The whole earth was covered with altars and

sacrificing priests. It is certain that in the second century the Holy Table came to be regarded as an altar [84] ($θυσιαστήριον$), and the celebration of the Holy Eucharist as a sacrifice. I cannot here attempt to decide the great controversy, whether this sacrificial idea was contained in the primitive institution of the Eucharist; let us suppose that, as is frequently alleged, the conception of sacrifice was brought in by external influences.[85] In this case, we may ask why it should be supposed that this great change is due to the influence of the Mysteries? For in the Mysteries sacrifice was by no means a distinctive part of the ceremonial, while in the public religions, whether Jewish or pagan, it formed the very essence of worship, to which everything else led up. If it is necessary to suppose external influences, surely it is most natural to refer the phenomena to those which were before the eyes of all men rather than to those which were performed in secret.

"It seems likely that the use of $δίπτυχα$—tablets commemorating benefactors or departed saints—was a continuation of a similar usage of the religious associations."[86] The word is so common in later Greek, and designated so familiar an object, that no argument can be drawn merely from its use by both pagans and Christians. Only a single instance is adduced by Dr. Hatch of its use in a pagan association, and that in the latter part of the second century, so that the reading of the names of persons to be commemorated from the folding tablets called diptychs can scarcely have been known as a conspicuous feature in pagan religious associations, and therefore (one would think) can hardly have been the cause of diptychs being introduced into Christian worship. That pagans did commemorate their dead, and that such commemorations were an important part of their religion, is well known, and this may perhaps have quickened the natural desire of Christians to remember their departed when they commemorated the death of Him, the first-born from the dead, who died and lived that He might be Lord both of dead and living. But the hypothesis is scarcely necessary to account for that which seems to spring naturally enough from the views of life and death prevalent in the early Church.

When we compare pagan and Christian Mysteries, we must take into account not only resemblances, or fancied resemblances, in particular points, but their general tone and influence. Were the pagan Mysteries in general purifying and ennobling forces? A modern writer [87] says that "the majority of them had the same aims as Christianity itself—the aim of worshipping a pure God, the aim of living a pure life, and the aim of cultivating the spirit of brotherhood." I am quite disposed to believe that this is in the main true. That they attempted to cover the ground which the Christian Church in time completely occupied, to provide purification for the impure, worship such as to raise in the soul a truly religious emotion and aspiration, and the hope of bliss in a future life, I have said already. I am sure I may say further that no candid inquirer believes that the Eleusinian Mysteries, at any rate, shared in as they were by practically all the citizens of no mean city, commended as they were by some of the noblest souls of the ancient

world, were debasing and degrading rites.
Cicero seems to regard the Mysteries of Eleusis
and Samothrace as means of learning the
secrets of nature rather than of the gods,[88] and
this we may believe was the prevalent opinion
with men of Cicero's class; but as civilising
institutions he thinks no praise too high for
them; the Mysteries were the source whence
gentleness and humanity flowed over men and
states which before were sunk in savagery
and rudeness.[89] An epigrammatist[90] of the time
of Augustus begs his friend, if he can travel
nowhere else, at least to go to Athens, that he
may see the solemn rites of Demeter. When
a law of a religious association bears on its
front, "Let no one enter the most venerable
assembly unless he be pure and pious and
good" (I use the words of Dr. Hatch),[91] we
have no right to doubt that it was really
intended to promote amendment of life. Yet
it would also be an error to suppose that the
words used had precisely the same meaning
which they have for Christians; no words have,
in fact, been more transformed by the spirit of
Christ. The law requires that the candidate

for admission should be ἀγαθός, εὐσεβής, ἁγνός.⁹²
Now ἀγαθός is the term constantly used in inscriptions to describe one who had done some service to the State; built some public edifice, perhaps, or given of his wealth in time of need. It means that the man was public-spirited and presumably well-born. It scarcely refers at all to the qualities which constitute what we should call goodness. εὐσεβής is also a word very often found in inscriptions, designating the man who fulfils exactly all the rites of his pagan cult. It scarcely indicates, unless by implication, the disposition of heart and mind which we call "pious" or "devout." The remaining word, ἁγνός, means "chaste." We know from other sources that the candidates for initiation were required to render themselves, formally and materially, pure and chaste by maintaining for a few days continence and abstinence from certain kinds of food. Of what we should call chastity the pagan world had little conception, and their purity much more resembled that of the Levitical than that of the Christian law. Still, the founders of Mysteries wished for purity in their disciples as they understood purity.

The same writer whom I have just quoted admits that "there were elements in some of [the Mysteries] from which Christianity recoiled, and against which the Christian Apologists used the language of strong invective."[93] But it is not only Christian Apologists who use the language of invective; a series of ethnic writers have also deplored the evils which, if not inherent in the Mysteries, at any rate clustered round them. It was probably inevitable that round the really venerable institutions there should spring up impostors who pretended to convey the benefits of initiation on easier terms. It is to such for the most part that the denunciations of ancient moralists apply. Socrates in Plato[94] says, with a certain irony, that they were clever fellows who invented the mystic saying that in the world beyond the grave the uninitiated should lie in the mire, while the initiated should dwell with the gods; but he himself holds that they only are truly initiated who have given themselves to right philosophy. And again he speaks with an accent of contempt of the heaven which was idly dreamed by the Orphic poet, a heaven of garlands and goblets, as if perpetual drunkenness were the meet reward for a life of virtue. He denounces the wandering Orpheotelestæ, who claimed by mere ceremonies and incantations to save men —nay, even to save the dead—from the consequences of their transgressions, in terms not very unlike those in which Luther denounced the vagabond vendors of indulgences.[95] In the Laws which he proposed for his ideal polity Plato forbids private cults altogether.[96] Demosthenes[97] thinks it worth while to cast it in the teeth of his great rival, that his mother had practised initiations, while Aeschines himself served as her acolythe. Plutarch,[98] a very religious man, admired the moral elevation which he found in the rites of Isis, but he has unbounded contempt for the hangers-on of Serapis worship, whom he regards as not less base than the emissaries of the Mater Deorum. The history of the word ὄργια, our "orgies," is not uninstructive. Denoting originally merely things done, with the connotation that they were done with a religious purpose, it came to designate in the first century after Christ certain frantic secret rites which were believed to be accompanied by great impurity, and that even in Athens itself, the seat of the most venerable Mysteries. There must have been some reason for the association of ὄργια with immorality.

I think it may be said that every Christian writer who speaks of the Mysteries while they were still celebrated, denounces them in no measured terms as promoting impurity. Nevertheless, as to a portion of their charges, it is evident that they confused mythology with worship. It is the crimes and immoralities of gods and goddesses, as they appeared in legend and poetry, which they especially attack; as Lobeck acutely observes, they had no doubt that gods who were believed to have acted foully were also foully worshipped.[99] But the inference will not hold, for we have reason to think that one object of the Mysteries was to veil under a decent covering of allegory such stories of the gods as shocked the more thoughtful worshippers. But another charge of Christian writers—that in some of the Mysteries at least indecent symbols were exhibited—is, I believe, not to be refuted. Yet even here we must not judge the pagans by a standard derived from many centuries of Christianity. When symbols which to us would be in the highest degree offensive were commonly seen in streets and in gardens, the exhibition of similar objects in the Mysteries did not imply any special depravity. All we can say is that, in this respect at least, the standard of purity in the initiated did not rise above that of the world about them. And this is probably true generally. Until Christ came, it may be doubted whether any religious association ever succeeded in raising its members greatly above the conventional standard of morality which prevailed among those with whom they lived.

But when we have made all possible allowance for the prejudices of Christian witnesses, we must remember that they wrote while the Mysteries were an existing force. Some of them, we know, had been initiated and knew of what they spoke. Some, as Clement and Origen, by no means decried paganism as a whole; it also, like Judaism, was a dispensation of God. They may not have attacked the Mysteries intelligently, but there must have been some reason for their attacking them at all. The special horror which they inspired cannot have been wholly without a cause. And we may be sure that the assembly of crowds of both sexes at nocturnal celebrations of an exciting kind cannot have been exactly favourable to purity. Even with the far greater restraints imposed by Christianity it was soon found that nocturnal assemblies of excited worshippers at the tomb of a saint were productive of evil.

Whatever may have been their influence, the ancient Mysteries are gone. They made their attempt, not probably a wholly vain attempt, to gild the life of man by the gleams of hope of a life to come, better, purer, and brighter than that which now we lead. But they were essentially a part of the old paganism, and as the antique culture died away the rites and customs which it brought forth faded and vanished also. In the third and fourth centuries after Christ we see it in its death-throes. Paganism is smitten with a senile decay, while youthful Christianity is strong with a god-given strength. Before the day-spring from on high the torches of the mystic rite pale their ineffectual fires. The darkness is passing away, and the true light already shineth. Earth-born clouds still hang round the Sun of Righteousness; clouds even in our own land where Christ has been preached for many generations; clouds darker still in the lands where the very name of Christ is unknown; yet we know that the dawn has begun; we know that the Day-spring from on high hath visited us; and we doubt not that it will shine more and more unto the perfect day.

NOTES

K

NOTES

1. I am quite aware of the difficulty, perhaps impossibility, of defining "life," and of the objections which have been raised to the employment of such terms as "vital force," and the like. The illustration in the text, however, does not depend upon any theory as to the nature and origin of life, but simply on the recognition of a property as to which all are agreed. "Every living body possesses the power of taking into its interior certain materials foreign to those composing its own substance, and of converting these into the materials of which its body is built up. This constitutes the process of "assimilation," and it is in virtue of this that living bodies *grow*" (H. Alleyne Nicholson, *Elements of Biology*, p. 2). The conclusions of Pasteur and Tyndall as to the production of life from life, and from no other source, seem to remain unshaken.

2. See, for instance, Justin Martyr, *Apologia*, i. c. 46; ii. 10, 13; Clement Alex., *Strom.* i. pp. 331, 337, ed. Potter; Origen *in Genesin*, Hom. xiv. c. 3. Lactantius, in a noteworthy passage (*Instit.* vii. 7), declares that almost all truth was to be found dispersed through the various philosophies, but that Christianity separated the good from the bad, and wrought it into an intelligible whole.

2*. Ernest Havet, *Le Christianisme et ses Origines*.

When M. Havet says (i. p. vi.) that "si nous étudions en elles-même la pensée Chrétienne et la vie Chrétienne, nous n'y trouverons guère que ce qu'il y avait dans la philosophie et dans la religion des Grecs-Romains, ou ce qui a dû en sortir naturellement par l'effet des influences sous lesquelles le monde s'est trouvé placé précisément vers la date de l'ère nouvelle," he states the case far too strongly; in fact, Christianity caused a revolution in thought and life; it did not derive its existence from the current religions and philosophies, however much it may have drawn from them. What Renan (*Études d'Hist. Rel.*, p. 188) says of the influence of Judaism on early Christianity is true also of the Hellenic influence: "On me montrerait en détail toutes les maximes de l'Évangile dans Moïse et les prophètes, que je maintiendrais encore que l'y a dans la doctrine du Christ un esprit nouveau et un cachet original." It is this "esprit nouveau" which M. Havet takes little account of. Edmund Spiess, in the Introduction to his *Logos Spermaticos* (Leipzig, 1871), gives a good account of the relation of pagan thought to Christianity.

3. Augustin, *Retractationes*, i. 13: "Res ipsa quae nunc religio Christiana nuncupatur erat apud antiquos nec defuit ab initio generis humani, quousque Christus veniret in carnem, unde vera religio quae jam erat coepit appellari Christiana."

4. *Essay* 24, "Of Innovation."

5. See De Tocqueville's *L'Ancien Régime et la Révolution*. English translation by H. Reeve.

6. On this point see Dr. H. A. A. Kennedy's excellent treatise on the *Sources of New Testament Greek* (Edinburgh, 1895).

7. *La religion Romaine d'Auguste aux Antonins*, vol. i. p. 72.

8. The statue at Paneas which Eusebius (*Hist. Eccl.* vii. 18) describes, was probably erected in honour of Hadrian or some other emperor, with the inscription, τῷ σωτῆρι. See Hefele's *Beiträge zur Kirchengeschichte*, ii. 257; Smith and Cheetham, *Dict. of Christ. Antiq.* i. 877. Wobbermin (*Kirchengeschichtliche Studien*, 15, 33, 105) points out that the gods of the Mysteries were commonly spoken of as σωτῆρες.

9. Abundant instances of the persistence of ancient harvest-customs may be seen in Mr. J. G. Frazer's *Golden Bough*.

10. In this it is not intended to deny that many of the Gnostic teachers were on the whole superior in literary cultivation to those of the Christians, or that they were able and imaginative, or that they loved a certain splendour in worship. Early Christian teachers recognised their ability and popular endowments. Origen speaks with respect of the Gnostic commentator Heracleon, though he does not accept his conclusions; and Jerome (on Hosea ii. 10; *Opera* vi. 1, 106 ed. Vall.) says: "Nullus potest haeresim struere nisi qui ardens ingenii est et habet dona naturae quae a deo artifice sunt creata; talis fuit Valentinus, talis Marcion, quos doctissimos legimus; talis Bardesanes, cujus etiam philosophi admirantur ingenium." What is maintained is that, with all its superficial Hellenism, the root-idea of Gnosticism is un-Hellenic. The notion of evil inherent in matter, so that the deity must be several times diluted before he can come in contact with it, is surely not Greek; Plato's demiurgus is something very different from the demiurgus of the Gnostics, though they probably

borrowed the term from him. Wobbermin, however, (*Kirchengeschichtliche Studien*, p. 73 *ff.*, supposes that both Plato and the Gnostics borrowed the word from the Orphic mysticism. Nor does the Gnostic appeal to an esoteric tradition harmonise with a philosophy which, like that of the Greeks, brought everything to the test of reason. It is Oriental. A. Harnack (*Dogmengeschichte*, i. 165) applies to Gnosticism the text, "The voice is Jacob's voice, but the hands are the hands of Esau," meaning to imply that Gnosticism, in spite of appearances, is at bottom Hellenic. I should have thought rather that, in spite of its Hellenic skin, it remained in substance Oriental. Its voice is the voice of the East.

11. S. H. Butcher, *Some Aspects of the Greek Genius*, p. 1 *f.*

12. After the time of Alexander the Great, says Schwegler (*History of Philosophy*, p. 143, Stirling's Trans.), "a feeling of unhappiness, of unappeasable longing, took the place of that fair unity between spirit and nature which had been characteristic of the better periods of Grecian political and intellectual life. A last desperate attempt to reach the alienated divine life . . by means of transcendent speculation and ascetic mortification, by means of ecstasy and swoon, was made by Neo-Platonism; it failed, and ancient philosophy sank in complete exhaustion, ruined in the attempt to conquer dualism. Christianity took up the problem."

13. Marquardt-Wissowa, *Römische Staatsverwaltung*, Bd. iii. p. 209 (2te Aufl.). The whole of Marquardt's treatise on *Das Sacralwesen* is highly instructive.

14. "Si haut qu'on remonte dans l'histoire de la race indo-européenne . . . on ne voit pas que cette race ait

jamais pensé qu'après cette courte vie tout fût fini pour l'homme. Les plus anciennes générations, bien avant qu'il y eût des philosophes, ont cru à une seconde existence après celle-ci. Elles ont envisagé la mort, non comme une dissolution de l'être, mais comme un simple changement de vie."—Fustel de Coulanges, *La Cité Antique*, c. i.

15. The terms commonly used by the Greeks to designate what we commonly call Mysteries were τελεταί, ὄργια, μυστήρια. In Latin the word "initia" is used. These Greek names were used generally for all kinds of mystic rites, purifications, atonements, and witchcrafts (see Lobeck, p. 89 *f.*), but in a more special sense for a particular class of institutions and festivals, including many rites, such as the Eleusinian in the older Hellenic period, and the Isiac under the Empire. The word τελετή occurs first in Hesiod (fr. 29, p. 211, ed. Goettling), where it is applied to initiation into the Bacchic Mysteries; ὄργια is used of the Eleusinian in the Homeric hymn to Demeter (273, 476); μυστήρια is found in somewhat later authorities, and is used specially of the Attic Eleusinia, in which μικρά and μεγάλα μυστήρια are distinguished. The word μυστήριον is akin to μύειν, to close the eyes or lips. μυεῖν and μυεῖσθαι are used to designate the initiating or being initiated into a mystic secret, which is called μυστήριον. The plural μυστήρια (first in Herod. ii. 51) is used sometimes for a particular assemblage of secret rites, regarded as a whole, sometimes for the objects of the secret worship, sometimes for the ritual acts themselves. The leading thought in μυστήρια and the kindred words is concealment from the uninitiated, and from this its derivatives in modern languages have come to connote something in itself obscure and difficult to comprehend, a notion which is not necessarily

contained in the Greek. In the New Testament a μυστήριον is a secret, something which is only known by being communicated, as opposed to things which are open to any one to discover. The revelation of Jesus Christ as the Saviour of the world, for instance, is μυστήριον χρόνοις αἰωνίοις σεσιγμένον φανερωθὲν δὲ νῦν (Rom. xvi. 25, 26), and to this sense probably all the instances occurring in the New Testament may be referred (see T. K. Abbott, *Essays chiefly on the Original Texts of Old and New Testament*, p. 88 *ff.*). Clement of Alexandria (*Protrept.* i. 10) says that the Baptist preached ἵνα τῆς ἀληθείας τὸ φῶς, ὁ λόγος τῶν προφητικῶν αἰνιγμάτων, τὴν μυστικὴν ἀπολύσηται σιωπὴν εὐαγγέλιον γενόμενος: and many other instances are found of the application of μυστήριον and its derivatives to the now published secret of the Gospel. Further, it is applied to the Christian sacraments, as being institutions not derived from natural reason, but founded by the divine Master for the use and benefit of those who are His; that is, revealed secrets; and also as being reserved, like many ancient rites, for the use of the initiated only. To take one instance out of thousands, it was evidently the common designation of the Eucharist when the Council of Laodicea (c. 7) permitted certain heretics, on reciting the orthodox Creed and receiving the Chrism, κοινωνεῖν τῷ μυστηρίῳ τῷ ἁγίῳ. And with the conception of divine ordination and of limitation to the use of the faithful was no doubt associated that of grace imparted in ways above human thought.

The word ὄργια, on the other hand, connected as it is with ἔργον, ἔοργα, as ἑορτή is with ἔρδω (Lobeck, p. 305, note c) designates in its strict acceptation ritual acts simply, without any notion of secrecy; but being especially applied to the frantic dances and gesticulations of the Bacchanals and the like, it acquired the sense which is perpetuated in our word "orgies." τελετή has also originally a general sense of something accomplished, but it came specially to designate the act, or series of acts, which gave a kind of consecration to the candidate, and fitted him for admission to the secret. And as such a consecration was regarded as freeing a man from the sins of his past life, τελεταί were often regarded as equivalent to purifications (see Plato on the Orpheotelestae, Demosthenes on Aeschines). τελετή also came into use among philosophers for initiation into the highest and most recondite truths which they had to teach (Lobeck, p. 124 *ff.*). If τελετή means completion, "initia" means beginnings, elements, or first principles. It is applied to rites which are regarded as the elements of, or the introduction to, a further revelation. So Cicero (*De Legibus*, ii. 14, 36) "initia ut appellentur, ita revera principia vitae cognovimus." Varro (*De Re Rustica*, iii. 1; in Pauly, *Real-Encycl.* v. 318) connects the word in a noteworthy manner with the worship of Ceres. Pointing out that agriculture is the foundation of domestic life and gentler manners, he adds, "cui consentaneum est quod initia vocantur potissimum ea quae Cereri fiunt sacra." We may say that in the words μυστήρια, ὄργια, τελεταί we have the leading characteristics of the Mysteries—secrecy, emotion, and edification.

There were also societies very nearly akin to the Mysteries called θίασοι and ἔρανοι. The former seem always to have been formed mainly for the purpose of worship, especially the worship of some deity not recognised by the State. The worshippers of Serapis in Athens, for instance, formed a private association for the cult of their god, and were called Σαραπιασταί. The ἔρανοι were frequently formed purely for civic and social ends, but in many of these also religious ceremonies occupied a prominent place. See Foucart, *Associations Religieuses chez les Grecs*, p. 2 *ff.*

16. Lobeck, *Aglaophamus*, p. 270.

17. References to the teaching in the Mysteries are found in the following passages:—

>   ὄλβιος ὅστις ἰδὼν ἐκεῖνα
>   κοίλαν εἶσιν ὑπὸ χθόνα·
>   οἶδεν μὲν βιότου τελευτὰν
>   οἶδεν δὲ διόσδοτον ἀρχάν·

Pindar, Fr. Ὀρῆνοι 8; p. 375 Donaldson.

>   ὡς τρισόλβιοι
>   κεῖνοι βροτῶν οἳ ταῦτα δερχθέντες τέλη
>   μολοῦσ' ἐς Ἀΐδου· τοῖς δὲ γὰρ μόνοις ἐκεῖ
>   ζῆν ἐστι, τοῖς δ' ἄλλοισι πάντ' ἐκεῖ κακά.

Sophocles, Fr. *Triptol.* 719 Dind. Compare *Oedip. Col.* 1050; Aristophanes, *Ranae*, 145 *ff.*

18. In Synesius, *Orat.* p. 48; Fragment 15 Rose.

19. Doubtless Welcker is right when he says (*Griech. Götterlehre*, ii. 536) that the essence of the Eleusinian rite was in the drama and its accompaniments; it was through it that the mystic effect was wrought. The very name "Epoptae," which designates those admitted to the highest degree of initiation, shows that the beholding of wondrous sights was that which constituted their privilege.

20. Lobeck (*Aglaophamus*, p. 47) compares the feelings of the newly initiated to those of the young Protestant Mortimer in Schiller's *Maria Stuart* when he was present for the first time at a stately act of Roman Catholic worship, in which, in

>   "die leuchtende Verklärung,
>   Das Herrlichste, das Höchste gegenwärtig
>   Vor den entzückten Sinnen sich bewegte."

21. One of the charges against Alcibiades was that he had parodied the Mysteries, and especially that he had shown the sacred objects to his boon companions (ἔχοντα στολὴν οἱάνπερ ἱεροφάντης ἔχων δεικνύει τὰ ἱερά, Plutarch, *Alcibiades*, 22). See further in Lobeck's *Aglaophamus*, p. 48 ff.

22. *Descriptio Graeciae*, 1. 38. 7. Similarly in Plutarch's *Symposiac*. (Problem 8), the conversation is broken off when it seems to touch on Pythagorean secrets, a Pythagorean being present. See Lobeck, *u.s.* 66 ff.

23. See J. G. Frazer, *The Golden Bough*.

24. In what I have said of Demeter, Persephone, and Dionysus I have generally followed Preller, *Demeter und Persephone*, and *Griechische Mythologie* (ed. Robert).

25. Demeter was commonly regarded by the Greeks as γῆ μήτηρ, the earth-mother, and the epithet which they applied to her—αὐξιθαλής, χλοηφόρος, καρποποιός, σταχυηφόρος, σιτοφόρος, and the like—show clearly that they thought of her as the fertile earth. See Max Müller, *Contributions to the Science of Mythology*, p. 535 f. (1897). This etymology of the ancient Greeks does not seem in itself improbable, as it is almost certain that the δᾶ found in Doric passages in tragedy represents γῆ. Another etymology, found in the *Etymologicon Magnum* (265, 54), and advocated by Ahrens, *Philologus*, xxii. 207 (1866), and by several other philologists after him, makes Δημήτηρ = Δημομήτηρ, mother of the community, which corresponds well with her epithet θεσμοφόρος. See Preller-Robert, *Griech. Mythol.* 747, n. 6. Another proposed etymology is from δηαί, Cretan form of ζειαί, barley. See Baumeister, *Denkmäler des klassischen Alterthums*, i. 411.

26. Eunapius, *Vitae Sophistarum*, p. 78, ed. Colon.

See Preller in Pauly's *Real-Encyclop.* iii. 88. The results of the most recent researches in Eleusis are to be found in Πρακτικὰ τῆς ἀρχαιολ. ἑταιρίας, 1883. Plan of the foundations in Baumeister's *Denkmäler*, i. 477.

27. There is an excellent account of the spread of the worship of Egyptian deities beyond Egypt by George Lafaye, *Histoire du culte des divinités d'Alexandrie hors de l'Égypte* (Paris, 1884). Foucart (*Recherches sur l'origine et la nature des mystères d'Eleusis*. Paris, 1895) contends that the Eleusinian Mysteries were derived from Egypt. His arguments are, however, by no means convincing as to the origin of the Mysteries, though they probably received some influence from Egypt in later times.

28. Among the numerous books on the ancient Egyptian religion, may be mentioned Le Page Renouf, *Lectures on the Origin and Growth of Religion, as illustrated by the Religion of Ancient Egypt* (Hibbert Lectures, 1879); J. Lieblein, *Egyptian Religion* (1884): H. Brugsch, *Religion und Mythologie der alten Ägypter*; E. Lefébvre, *L'Étude de la religion Égyptienne*, in *Revue de l'histoire des religions*, 1886, vol. ii.

29. Tibullus, i. 7, 25 *ff.* Brugsch, *Religion und Mythologie der alten Ägypter*, p. 621, referred to by J. G. Frazer, *Golden Bough*, i. 305 *f.* Servius on Virgil, *Georg.* i. 166. Plutarch (*Isis and Osiris*, 35; i. 446 Dübner) says that the Τιτανικά and Νυκτέλια in the Bacchic cult correspond to τοῖς λεγομένοις Ὀσίριδος διασπασμοῖς καὶ ταῖς ἀναβιώσεσι καὶ παλιγγενεσίαις.

30. Diodorus Sic. *Bibliotheca*, i. 51.

31. On union with Osiris, see Chantepie de la Saussaye, *Religionsgeschichte*, i. 291 *f.*; Wallis Budge, *The Papyrus of Ani*.

32. These formularies are contained in the *Book of the Dead*. The best text is that published by Édouard Naville, *Das ägyptische Todtenbuch der xviii. bis xx. Dynastie* (Berlin, 1886), well reviewed by Miss A. B. Edwards in the *Academy*, 10th September 1887. See also A. E. Wallis Budge, *Dwellers on the Nile*, ch. 9, and *The Papyrus of Ani*.

33. See Seyffert-Nettleship-Sandys, *Dictionary*, p. 578.

34. Plutarch, *De Iside et Osiride*, c. 66; p. 461 Dübner. See Lafaye, *Divinités d'Égypte*, p. 71.

35. *Metamorphoses*, lib. xi. c. 2, 5.

36. The work of T. Fabri, *De Mithrae dei solis invicti apud Romanos cultu* (1883), contains a valuable collection of the principal documents relating to Mithraism, and a list of Mithraic inscriptions. A still more complete collection is Cumont's *Textes et monuments figurés relatifs aux mystères de Mithra*. An account of the principal Mithraic remains in England may be found in C. Wellbeloved's *Eburacum* (York, 1842).

37. "Baudissin hat mit reichem und sorgfältig geordnetem Material den Satz erhärten wollen, das bei den Semiten die Bäume nur als Zeichen der in der Natur sich offenbarenden lebenserzeugenden Gotteskraft verehrt wurden. ... Wenn man nun auch diese erklärung nicht allgemein auf jeden Baumcultus anwenden kann, so ist sie doch gewiss für manche Erscheinungen die richtige. ... Die Vorstellung der Verwandschaft zwischen dem animalischen und dem vegetabilischen Leben und Wachsthum ... spricht sich aus in den Mythen welche Menschen aus Pflanzen oder Bäumen entstehen lassen."—Chantepie de la Saussaye, *Religionsgeschichte*, i. 65.

38. "A belief in another life is found among the lowest, as among the highest of human beings. Here the wish has

clearly been father to the thought, and we need not look further to account for whatever coincidences may be pointed out. But when we find descriptions of heaven and hell, with punishments and rewards almost, nay altogether, identical, what shall we say? Surely no more than that what was possible in the South was possible in the North. What was possible in India was possible in other countries also; what occurred to the minds of Indian *Rishis* may have occurred to the minds of Pythagoras and Pherekydes also." —Max Müller, *Contributions*, 832 *f.*

When the conception of the continued existence of the soul in another region is once reached, the further idea of a judgment of souls, of the blessedness of the good, and the punishment of the bad, is not far off. We find it from the most ancient times in Egypt, and it may have been thence that it was diffused in Europe; but the supposition is not necessary.

39. Tatian, *Oratio adv. Graecos*, c. 29.

40. See Anrich, *Mysterienwesen*, pp. 37, 47. Wobbermin (*Studien*, 105) says well on this subject, that "the moral seriousness of the New Testament conception of σωτηρία, its relation on the one hand to the power and dominion of sin, on the other to the redeeming love of the heavenly Father, has little or no analogy in the Greek Mysteries."

41. Preller in Pauly, *Real-Encyclop.* v. 336.

42. Renan, *Études d'hist. relig.* 58.

43. E. Hatch, *Hibbert Lectures*, p. 294.

44. Lobeck, after noticing the application to philosophy of terms derived from the Mysteries, says very justly (*Aglaophamus*, p. 130): "Has omnes similitudines si ad amussim exigere et, quidquid de una aliqua re, quae cum

mysteriis comparatur, praedicari potest, illico ad ea ipsa transferre velimus, ad postremum eo deveniemus, ut initiatis non Theologiae solum rationem, sed quasi quandam artium et scientiarum encyclopaediam, ut nunc loqui solent, traditam esse confiteamur." See Anrich, *Mysterienwesen*, p. 65.

45. Cicero, *Verr.* iv. 59, c. 132: "Hi qui hospites ad ea quae visenda sunt ducere solent et unumquodque ostendere; quos illi mystagogos vocant." See Lobeck, p. 30.

46. Hatch, *Hibbert Lectures*, p. 295.

47. Anrich, *Mysterienwesen*, p. 120 *ff.* The question, whether the words φωτισμός and σφραγίς were applied by the pagans to the Mysteries, is discussed at some length by Wobbermin (*Studien*, 144 *ff.*), who believes that the words "came to be used to designate Christian baptism not without the influence of the Mysteries." He does not, however, produce any instance of the direct application of the word φωτισμός to pagan Mysteries, though there is no doubt of the fact that the sacred objects and acts were displayed to the initiated under a brilliant light. In the case of σφραγίς it does not seem to have occurred to him that the use of the word "signatae" in a pagan inscription of the third century hardly proves that the Christian use of σφραγίς by (*e.g.*) Hermas was derived from that of paganism; or that Tertullian's application of the word "signare," with which he was familiar in the Christian Church, to a pagan rite, does not prove that the pagans of that time so applied it; or that a passage of Suidas, written in the eleventh century, in which no ancient authority is quoted, and which requires amending before it can be used, does not throw much light on the usage of the second century.

48. *Orat.* 40, p. 639.

49. Justin Martyr is generally ridiculed for his statement that "wicked dæmons" imitated the Eucharist in the Mysteries of Mithras. But in truth, though the Mithraic worship is no doubt older than Christianity, it is by no means impossible that in the second century after Christ the Mithraists may have assimilated their forms to those of the Christians.

50. Hatch, *Hibbert Lectures*, p. 293.

51. Clement Alexand. *Protrept.* ii. c. 22; Euseb. *Dem. Evang.* v. Prooem. c. 17; *Praeparatio*, xv. 1. It must be said, however, that many of the passages commonly cited relate rather to the licentiousness of the pagan mythology in general than to the Mysteries in particular.

52. Schürer, *Geschichte des Jüdischen Volkes*, ii. p. 357. "Es ist vor allem zu beachten, dass das Hauptzweck dieser Sabbatversammlungen in der Synagoge nicht der Gottesdienst im engern Sinne, d. h. nicht die Anbetung war, sondern die religiöse Unterweisung." Josephus tells us (*Bell. Jud.* vii. 3. 3) that the Jews in Antioch attracted to their assemblies πολὺ πλῆθος Ἑλλήνων, and there are many similar testimonies. Schürer, *u.s.* p. 558 *ff.*

53. Pliny, *Epist.* x. 96 [al. 97].

54. Chrysostom in the 3rd Homily on Lazarus (*Opera* v. 652, ed. Montfaucon) speaks as if his auditors possessed, and could read, the scriptures.

55. Basil, *De Spiritu Sancto*, c. 66: τὰ τῆς ἐπικλήσεως ῥήματα ἐπὶ τῇ ἀναδείξει τοῦ ἄρτου τῆς εὐχαριστίας καὶ τοῦ ποτηρίου τῆς εὐλογίας τίς τῶν ἁγίων ἐγγράφως ἡμῖν καταλέλοιπεν;

56. Origen, *c. Celsum*, i. 7. Dr. Hatch does not seem to have noticed this passage, though he refers to this chapter, p. 293, n. 1.

57. The same feeling also influenced pagans. "Parem noxam contraherent aures et linguae illae temerariae curiositatis," says Apuleius, *Metam.* xi. 23.

58. See Suicer, *Thesaurus*, s.v. κατηχέω; F. X. Funk, in *Theol. Quartalschrift* (Tübingen), 1883, p. 41 *ff.*

59. Lobeck, *Aglaophamus*, p. 40. "Gradatim sacra percipi dicit et ex intervallo. Quid ad rem? Nemo non eo quo intendit per gradus pervenit."

60. Hatch, *Hibbert Lectures*, p. 294.

60*. Jerome (*ad Laetam, Opp.* i. 672, ed. Vall.), and apparently Jerome alone, gives the names of (seemingly) eight grades of Mithraic initiation—Corax, Nymphus, Miles, Leo, Perses, Helios, Dromo, Pater—but the interpretation of the passage is very doubtful. The *Corpus Inscr. Lat.* vi. 749-753 proves the existence of six classes, Leontica, Persica, Heliaca, Patrica, Gryfu, Hierocoracica. Tertullian mentions the grade of Miles (*De Corona*, c. 15). See Anrich, *Mysterienwesen*, 45, note 3. Nonnus (Migne's *Patrol. Gracc.* xxxvi. 989; quoted by Fabri, p. 62) speaks of the trials (κολάσεις), through which the postulants had to pass, as trials by fire and frost, by hunger and thirst, by much wayfaring, and such like; and of such, he says, there were eighty. Such trials had obviously no resemblance to graduated instruction. (See further *u. s.* 1009-1012; 1072).

61. *Mathemat.* i. p. 18 (ed. Bull.), quoted by Lobeck, p. 38 *f.*

62. Clement's words are: τῶν μυστηρίων τῶν παρ. Ἕλλησιν ἄρχει μὲν τὰ καθάρσια, καθάπερ καὶ ἐν τοῖς βαρβάροις τὸ λουτρόν. μετὰ ταῦτα δ' ἐστὶ τὰ μικρὰ μυστήρια διδασκαλίας ὑπόθεσιν ἔχοντα καὶ προπαρασκευῆς τῶν μελλόντων. *Strom.* v. cc. 71, 72, p. 689, Potter.

The meaning of this passage is discussed by Lobeck, p. 140 *ff.*

63. See Lobeck, p. 188 *ff.* Lucius in Apuleius (*Metam.* xi. 28), supposed to be a very devout worshipper, fasted from animal food ten days.

64. Rohde's *Psyche*, p. 368.

65. Foucart, *Associations religieuses chez les Grecs*, 124 *ff.*, 165 *ff.*

66. Theophrastus, *Characteres*, 30 [*al.* 17]; Plutarch, *De Superstitione*, cc. 3, 6, 12, 13. Josephus (*c. Apion.* ii. 22) saw the resemblance between the abstinences of the pagans and those of the Jews, except in that what was with the latter regular was with the former occasional and for a few days only.

67. Apuleius, *Metam.* xi. 6, 21, 33.

68. *De Praescriptionibus*, c. 40: "Tingit et ipse [diabolus] quosdam, utique credentes et fideles suos; expiationem [*al.* expositionem] delictorum de lavacro repromittit, et, si adhuc memini Mithrae, signat ille in frontibus milites suos." (Leopold's text.)

69. *De Mithrae apud Rom. cultu*, p. 22: "Falsa autem esse narrata constat. Valde enim abhorret a cultu arcano initiatos signis frontibus affixis significare."

70. *Aglaophamus*, p. 188.

71. *de Symbolo*, c. 2.

72. Hatch, *Hibbert Lectures*, p. 298.

73. Plautus, *Miles Gloriosus*, iv. 2. 26; Clement Alexand. *Protrept.* c. 2, §§ 15, 21, 22; Firmicus Maternus, *De Errore Profan. Gent.* c. 18. Apuleius says (*De Magia*, c. 55): "Sacrorum pleraque initia in Graecia participavi. Eorum quaedam signa et monumenta tradita mihi a sacerdotibus sedulo conservo." This clearly refers to

material objects. When in another passage (c. 56) he says, "si quis forte adest eorundem solemnium mihi particeps, signum dato et audiat licet quae ego adservem," it seems more probable that he refers to a password or gesture. See Lobeck, 23 *ff.*, 705 *ff.*; Anrich, 29, 30.

74. Hatch, *Hibbert Lectures*, p. 298.

75. *Metam.* xi. 23.

76. See Smith and Cheetham's *Dict. of Chr. Antiq.* p. 157.

77. Hatch, *Hibbert Lectures*, p. 298.

78. Percy Gardner, *The Origin of the Lord's Supper*, p. 7.

79. Gardner, *u.s.*, p. 17.

80. The κυκεών was a kind of porridge. In Homer's time (*Il.* xi. 638 *ff.*) it was made of barley-meal, goats'-milk cheese, and Pramnian wine; to which Circe added honey and magical herbs (*Od.* x. 234 *ff.*). But the κυκεών in the Homeric hymn to Demeter (208 *f.*), which is almost certainly identical with that administered in the Mysteries, is composed of barley-meal, water, and pennyroyal, without wine. The articles contained in the mystic chest are enumerated by Clement (*Protrept.* ii. 2, § 22), who had himself been initiated into several Mysteries (Euseb. *Praepar. Evang.* ii. 2, § 35), as follows: οἶαι δὲ καὶ αἱ κίσται αἱ μυστικαί; (δεῖ γὰρ ἀπογυμνῶσαι τὰ ἄγια αὐτῶν καὶ τὰ ἄρρητα ἐξειπεῖν). οὐ σησαμαῖ ταῦτα καὶ πυραμίδες καὶ τολύπαι καὶ πόπανα πολυόμφαλα χόνδροι τε ἁλῶν καὶ δράκων, ὄργιον Διονύσου Βασσάρου; οὐχὶ δὲ ῥοιαὶ πρὸς τοῖσδε καὶ κράδαι, νάρθηκές τε καὶ κιττοί; πρὸς δὲ καὶ φθοῖς καὶ μήκωνες; ταῦτ᾽ ἔστιν αὐτῶν τὰ ἄγια καὶ πρόσετι τῆς Θέμιδος τὰ ἀπόρρητα σύμβολα, ὀρίγανον, λύχνος, ξίφος, κτεὶς γυναικεῖος, ὅ ἐστιν, εὐφήμως καὶ μυστικῶς εἰπεῖν, μόριον

γυναικεῖον. I have adopted the conjecture approved by Lobeck, κράδαι for κραδίαι. In other respects the text is that of Klotz's ed. vol. i. p. 19. Sesame-cakes, wheat-cakes (if πυραμίς is formed from πυρός), balls (if they were farinaceous, which is doubted), round cakes, grains of salt, pomegranates, the cakes called φθοῖς, poppy-heads, and marjoram, might no doubt be tasted, though the effect, if they were all tasted at one time, might not be agreeable. Twigs of the fig-tree, stems of the giant-fennel, and ivy-leaves, might be more refractory. The hand-lamp, the sword, and the other object mentioned, must have been altogether impracticable. Whether there is anything in this strange mingle-mangle which can by any possibility have suggested the simple bread and wine of the Holy Communion my readers will judge. Lobeck (*Aglaoph.* p. 703) should be consulted on the passage; Anrich (p. 29) refers to O. Jahn, *Hermes*, 3, 228. It may perhaps be doubted whether writers on the Mysteries have taken sufficient account of the atmosphere of jest and sport which surrounded at any rate the Eleusinian. And yet the word γεφυρίζειν perpetuates the memory of the slang in which the votaries indulged as they passed in procession to Eleusis; and the bathing of a multitude in the sea can scarcely have been a very solemn spectacle. If it were not for Eusebius's statement that Clement was initiated, we might easily imagine that his ἔπιον τὸν κυκεῶνα κτλ was a mere jingle current in the streets of Athens, not to be taken more seriously than similar phrases in Aristophanes.

81. *Hibbert Lectures*, p. 298.

82. In Cudworth's *True Notion of the Lord's Supper*, *Works*, iv. p. 225, ed. Birch.

83. *Introduction to the History of Religion*, p. 414. It

may be observed that the "Cyprian" of this extract is not the well-known bishop of Carthage, but (seemingly) Cyprian of Antioch.

84. See Smith and Cheetham's *Dictionary of Christian Antiq.* p. 60.

85. There is a passage respecting sacrifice in Dr. Hatch's *Hibbert Lectures* (p. 300), which is so curious as to be worth citing. "There is one more symbolical rite in that early Easter sacrament, the mention of which is often suppressed — a lamb was offered on the altar." The general authority given for the whole passage is "Mabillon, *Com. Praev. ad Ord. Rom. ; Musaeum Ital.* II. xciv.," and on the passage just cited, it is noted that this sacrifice "was one of the points to which the Greeks objected in the discussions of the ninth century." Mabillon himself, in the passage referred to, points out that the Greek charge, that the Pope offered a lamb on the altar, arose from a mere blunder, the blessing of a lamb for eating having been taken for an offering. The lamb was in fact roasted before it was brought for the papal benediction (Migre's *Patrologia Lat.* lxxviii. 907, 1044). Pope Nicholas I. (in Hardouin's *Concilia*, v. 309 D) says that this sacrifice is a lie of the Greeks ; such a lie, adds Aeneas, Bishop of Paris (*Ib.* 318 A), as only a fool would believe. It was therefore certainly not practised "as late as the ninth century" in which Nicholas and his correspondent lived.

86. Hatch, *Hibbert Lectures*, p. 305.

87. Hatch, *u.s.* p. 291.

88. Cicero, *Nat. Deor.* i. 42, § 119 : "Omitto Eleusina . . praetereo Samothraciam," in which "rerum magis natura cognoscitur quam deorum."

89. *Verr.* v. 72, c. 187 : "Ceres et Libera, quarum

sacra longe maximis et occultissimis caerimoniis continentur, a quibus initia vitae atque victus, morum, legum, mansuetudinis, humanitatis hominibus ac civitatibus data ac dispertita esse dicuntur."

De Legibus, ii. p. 14, § 36: "Quum multa eximia divinaque videntur Athenae tuae peperisse atque in vita hominum attulisse, tum nihil melius illis mysteriis quibus ex agresti immanique vita exculti ad humanitatem et mitigati sumus."

90. Krinagoras in *Anthol. Palat.* xi. 42—

ὄφρ' ἂν ἐκείνη
Δήμητρος μεγάλας νύκτας ἴδῃς ἱερῶν.

91. *Hibbert Lectures*, p. 291.

92. Foucart, *Associations religieuses*, p. 146 *ff*. I have taken Foucart's reading, ἁγνός for ἅγιος. On these words see Wobbermin, 39, 59 *ff.*, 149.

93. Hatch, *Hibbert Lectures*, 291.

94. *Phaedo*, 69 A.

95. *Republic*, 363 C, 365 A.

96. *Leges*, 910 C.

97. Demosthenes, *Parapresbeia*, §§ 199, 249.

98. See Foucart, *Ass. rel.* 169 *f.* 179, and note 15 above.

99. Lobeck, *Aglaophamus*, p. 297: "Non dubitabant quin ii turpiter colerentur qui multa turpiter fecisse crederentur."

THE END

www.ingramcontent.com/pod-product-compliance
Lightning Source LLC
Chambersburg PA
CBHW022117160426
43197CB00009B/1065